MAKING OUT IN KOREAN

Revised Edition Expanded

by **Peter Constantine**
2nd edition revised by **Gene Baik**
3rd edition revised by **Laura Kingdon and Chris Backe**

TUTTLE Publishing
Tokyo | Rutland, Vermont | Singapore

Published by Tuttle Publishing, an imprint of Periplus Editions (HK) Ltd.

www.tuttlepublishing.com

Copyright @ 1995 Peter Constantine
Copyright @ 2004, 2014 Periplus Editions (HK) Ltd.
Illustrations by Dami Lee
All rights reserved.

ISBN 978-0-8048-4354-6

Distributed by:

North America, Latin America & Europe
Tuttle Publishing
364 Innovation Drive, North Clarendon VT 05759-9436, USA
Tel: 1 (802) 773 8930 | Fax: 1 (802) 773 6993
info@tuttlepublishing.com
www.tuttlepublishing.com

Japan
Tuttle Publishing
Yaekari Building 3F, 5-4-12 Osaki, Shinagawa-ku,
Tokyo 141-0032, Japan
Tel: (81) 3 5437 0171 | Fax: (81) 3 5437 0755
sales@tuttle.co.jp
www.tuttle.co.jp

Asia Pacific
Berkeley Books Pte. Ltd.
61 Tai Seng Avenue #02-12, Singapore 534167
Tel: (65) 6280-1330 | Fax: (65) 6280-6290
inquiries@periplus.com.sg
www.periplus.com

20 19 18 17 16
8 7 6 5 4 3   1607RR

Printed in China

TUTTLE PUBLISHING® is a registered trademark of Tuttle Publishing,
a division of Periplus Editions (HK) Ltd.

Contents

INTRODUCTION 7

1 **What's Up?** 15

2 **Basic Phrases** 27

3 **Got a Minute?** 35

4 **Hey There!** 41

5 **Look at That!** 49

6 **Coming and Going** 53

7 **Eat, Drink, Be Merry!** 59

8 **I Like It!** 73

9 **Curses and Insults** 83

10 **Party Talk** 95

11 **Getting Serious** 113

12 **On the Phone** 117

13 **On the Computer** 123

14 **Lover's Language** 143

15 **Farewell** 157

Introduction

Making Out in Korean introduces a colloquial form of spoken Korean, that you would not learn in any formal language course. It gives you an edge when maneuvering through the ins and outs of everyday life in Korean.

Unlike English, Korean has several speech levels that are formally codified. Age, social standing or the degree of intimacy you have with the person being addressed determines the level of politeness you should adopt. The different speech levels are marked by the verb endings placed at the end of sentences. Needless to say, you are required to use the polite form with strangers, your seniors and to those of a higher social status. However, as your relationship with them develops, a more relaxed and casual form of the language may be adopted.

Making Out in Korean presents the intimate and colloquial speech level of Korean that is often used among very close friends, including couples. This book contains "street-Korean" in addition to derogatory and vulgar expressions to enrich your spoken Korean!

Apart from the *Curses and Insults* section, any words requiring caution are marked and coupled with explanations to avoid misuse. Although most of this phrase book adopts an intimate and colloquial style of speech, selected expressions are presented in the polite (informal) form, when necessary, and are marked in brackets. The polite (informal) form of

Korean is achieved by attaching **-yo** at the end of intimate speech forms, which usually end in **-a** or **-eo**.

Care should be taken not to jump the gun before a relationship has matured. Using an informal or vulgar speech level in the wrong social context would be considered extremely insulting to a Korean person. To be on the safe side, refrain from adopting such levels of speech until the other party initiates it or both parties have reached a mutual agreement to do so.

BASIC GRAMMAR

The Korean language follows the word order of Subject-Object-Verb as opposed to the word order (Subject-Verb-Object) of English. Verbs are placed at the end of sentences, a position that reflects its importance in Korean grammar.

I am going to school.   **hak-kyo ga.** (Statement)
hahk-kkyo gah.
학교 가.

Literally means "School go."

Another salient feature of spoken Korean is that any element of the sentence may be omitted except the verb as long as you can clearly gather from the context what is being talked about. As a result, a single verb can be a complete sentence in Korean as indicated by the third example below.

Go to school!   **hak-kyo ga!** (Command)
hahk-kkyo gah!
학교 가.

Literally means "School go."

Let's go to school.   **hak-kyo ga.** (Suggestion)
hahk-kkyo gah.
학교 가.

Literally means "School go."

Are you going?   **ga?** (Question)
gah?
가?

Literally means "Go?"

Going to school!   **hak-kyo ga.** (Exclamation)
    (You're joking!)   *hahk-kyo gah.*
학교 가!

In Korean, the same sentence structure can be used for both sentences and statements. The following examples illustrate that by merely substituting the question word "where" with "school" changes a question into a declarative statement:

Where are you   <u>**erdi**</u> **ga?** (Question)
    going?   *uhdee gah?*
어디 가?

Literally means "Where go?"

I am going to school.   <u>**hak-kyo**</u> **ga.** (Statement)
hahk-kyo gah.
학교 가.

Literally means "School go."

Broadly speaking, expressions in the intimate form of speech can be converted into the polite (informal) form by simply adding **-yo** at the end, which usually end in **-a** or **-eo**:

> **hak-kyo ga.** (Intimate level of speech)
> *hahk-kyo gah.*
> 학교 가.

Literally means "School go."

> **hak-kyo gayo.** (Informal polite level of speech)
> *hahk-kyo gahyo.*

Literally means "School go."

READING ROMANIZED KOREAN

Two systems are used to show the pronunciation of the Korean phrases in the ordinary English alphabet.

The upper line on the right of the page follows the official Revised Romanization of Korean prepared and authorized by the Korean government in 2000. The letters used in this transcription have to be pronounced in a certain way only: they should not be treated like the letters in English which have different sounds in different words, for example the **a** in "apple," "father," "syllable" and "date."

Because it can at first be quite difficult for English speakers to read romanized Korean correctly, an approximate phonetic equivalent, designed to reflect the closest English equivalent to each Korean sound, is given in a second line underneath the official transcription of each phrase. Where necessary, a hyphen (-) is used to mark a syllable boundary so that any confusion in pronunciation is avoided.

Each phase is also written in Korean script under the Romanized and phonetic phrases on the right of the page, so that if you have difficulty in making yourself understood by following the romanized versions you can show the book to the person you're talking to and they will be able to read what you mean.

CONSONANTS

(1) Simple consonants

ㄱ g, k	ㄴ n	ㄷ d, t	ㄹ r, l	ㅁ m
ㅂ b, p	ㅅ s	ㅇ ng	ㅈ j	ㅊ ch
ㅋ k	ㅌ t	ㅍ p	ㅎ h	

(2) Double consonants

ㄲ kk	ㄸ tt	ㅃ pp	ㅆ ss	ㅉ jj

Most of the consonants are pronounced as in English except the tensed (double) consonants.

Double Consonants

There isn't much difficulty in pronouncing romanized Korean except for the tensed (double) consonants that require a relatively strong muscular effort in the vocal organs without the expulsion of air.

English	Korean	Approximate in English
kk	ㄲ	as in "s<u>k</u>i," "s<u>k</u>y"
tt	ㄸ	as in "s<u>t</u>eak," "s<u>t</u>ing"
pp	ㅃ	as in "s<u>p</u>eak," "s<u>p</u>y"
ss	ㅆ	as in "<u>s</u>ea," "<u>s</u>ir"
jj	ㅉ	as in "bri<u>dg</u>e," "mi<u>d</u>get" (similar to a tutting sound in an exhaling way)

VOWELS

(1) Simple vowels

ㅏ a	ㅓ eo	ㅗ o	ㅜ u	ㅡ eu
ㅣ i	ㅐ ae	ㅔ e		

(2) Diphthongs

ㅑ ya	ㅕ yeo	ㅛ yo	ㅠ yu	ㅒ yae
ㅖ ye	ㅘ wa	ㅙ wae	ㅝ wo	ㅞ we
ㅢ ui	ㅚ oe	ㅟ wi		

English	Korean	Approximate in English
a *(ah)*	ㅏ	as in "f<u>a</u>ther"
eo *(er)*	ㅓ	as in "b<u>o</u>x" or "c<u>u</u>t" (halfway between the two)
o *(aw)*	ㅗ	as in "f<u>a</u>ll"
u *(oo)*	ㅜ	as in "b<u>oo</u>"
eu *(oh)*	ㅡ	as in "tak<u>e</u>n"
i *(ee)*	ㅣ	as in "s<u>ee</u>"
ae *(a)*	ㅐ	as in "t<u>a</u>d" (often becomes more like the **ay** in "w<u>ay</u>")

e *(e)*	ㅔ	as in "b<u>e</u>g"
oe *(we)*	ㅚ	as in "<u>we</u>lcome"
ya *(yah)*	ㅑ	as in "<u>ya</u>rn"
yeo *(yaw)*	ㅕ	as in "<u>yo</u>nder"
yo *(yo)*	ㅛ	as in "<u>yo</u>gurt" (said with a slight pull)
yu *(yu)*	ㅠ	as in "<u>yu</u>le" (said with a slight pull)
yae *(ya)*	ㅒ	as in "<u>ya</u>k"
ye *(ye)*	ㅖ	as in "<u>ye</u>s"
wa *(wah)*	ㅘ	as in "<u>wa</u>tch"
wae *(wa)*	ㅙ	as in "<u>wa</u>y"
wo *(wo)*	ㅝ	as in "<u>wo</u>nderful"
wi *(wi)*	ㅟ	as in the "<u>wee</u>d"
ui *(ooe)*	ㅢ	this is a combination of 2 sounds -**u** as in "p<u>u</u>ll" followed by **ee** as in "<u>see</u>." It's kind of like 'oui' in French.

The Korean writing system, Han-geul (한글) demands that any **written** syllable must begin with a consonant. This means that even when a syllable begins with a vowel sound (the syllable contains no spoken consonants) you have to start the syllable with the consonant ㅇ, which has no sound.

1

What's Up?

POLITE GREETINGS

How are you?	**annyeonghaseyo?** *ahn-nyawng-hah-seyo?* 안녕하세요?
I'm fine, thanks. And you?	**ne, annyeonghaseyo?** *ne, ahn-nyawng-hah-seyo?* 네, 안녕하세요?

Annyeonghaseyo? 안녕하세요? is a greeting that asks about the other person's well-being or good health. This expression can be used at any time of the day as "Good morning," "Good afternoon," "Good evening," "Hi," "Hello," or "How's it going?" The common response is simply **ne, annyeonghaseyo?** 네, 안녕하세요?.

How do you do?	**cheo-eum boep-kket-
	   sseumnida.**
	*chuh-um bwep-kke-sseum-
	   nee-dah.*
	처음 뵙겠습니다.

What's new?	**byeollil eop-jjiyo?** *byulleel up-jyo?* 별일 없지요?
—Nothing much.	**geujeo geuraeyo.** *geu-juh geu-rayo.* 그저 그래요.
—Things are hard.	**jom himdeureoyo.** *chohm him-deul-uhyo.* 좀 힘들어요.
—Things are busy.	**jom bappayo.** *chohm bah-ppah-yo.* 좀 바빠요.
How have you been?	**yojeum eotteoke jinaeseyo?** *yo-johm uh-ttoh-kay jeeneh- say-yo?* 요즘 어떻게 지내세요?
—I've been fine, thanks.	**jal jinaeyo.** *chahl jeenayo.* 잘 지내요.

CASUAL GREETINGS BETWEEN CLOSE FRIENDS

How are you doing?	**jal isseosseo?** *chahl iss-uss-oh?* 잘 있었어?
Yo, what's up?	**ya, jal isseonnya?** *yah, chahl iss-uht-nyah?* 야, 잘 있었나?

Dude, what's up?	**saekki, jal isseonnya?***
	sakkee, chahl iss-uht-nyah?
	새끼, 잘 있었냐?
	jasik, jal isseonnya?*
	jah-sheek, chahl iss-uht-nyah?
	자식, 잘 있었냐?

*Saekki "baby animal" and **jasik** "human baby" are used in Korean slang the way "asshole" is used in American English. When said to one's closest friends, they can be expressions of affection—but handle with care.

How've you been?	**eotteoke jinaesseo?**
	uh-toh-kay jiness-uh?
	어떻게 지냈어?
—I'm fine.	**jal isseosseo.**
	chahl jinessuh.
	잘 있었어.
Have you been doing OK?	**jal jinaesseo?**
	chahl jinessuh?
	잘 지냈어?
—Yeah, man!	**geurae, i jasiga!**
	geurae, i jashigah!
	그래, 이 자식아!

Handle with care.

Where did you go?	**eodi gasseosseo?**
	uh-dee gahssuss-uh?
	어디 갔었어?
It's been a while.	**oraenmaniya.**
	awren-mahnee-yah.
	오랜만이야.

—Yeah!

geurae!
geu-ray!
그래!

—Yeah, it's been ages.

geurae, oraenmaniya.
geu-rae, awren-mahnee-yah.
그래, 오랜만이야.

How's Peter/Mary?

Peter/Mary jal isseo?
Peter/Mary chahl isso?
피터/메리 잘 있어?

—Yeah, Peter/ Mary is fine.

eung, (Peter/Mary) jal isseo.
eung, (Peter/Mary) chahl isso.
응, (피터/메리) 잘 있어.

The subject is often omitted when it is clearly understood from the context. 응 (*eung*) is very often used in casual conversation to agree with something the other person has said. It's said a lot like a grunt.

How are Peter and Mary?

Peter hago Mary jal isseo?
Peter hahgo Mary chahl isso?
피터하고 메리 잘있어?

—Yeah, Peter and Mary are fine.

eung, (Peter hago Mary) jal isseo.
eung, (Peter hah-gaw Mary) chahl isso.
응,(피터하고 메리)
잘 있어.

Anything new with Peter/Mary?

Peter/Mary byeollil eopseo?
Peter/Mary byullil upso?
피터/메리 별일 없어?

—Yeah, he/she's
doing fine.

eung, byeollil eopseo.
eung, byullil upso.
응, 별일 없어.

—Yeah, he/she's OK.

eung, jal jinae.
eung, chahl jee-nay.
응, 잘 지내.

—Yeah, he/she's
doing so-so.

eung, geujeo geurae.
eung, geu-juh geuray.
응, 그저 그래.

What's wrong, man?

wae geurae, imma?
wa geu-ray, eem-mah.
왜 그래, 임마?

Handle with care.

Keep in mind as well that 임마 (*eem-mah*) is a swear word used
by men and will sound very coarse and weird coming from a
woman.

—Nothing's wrong
with me.

amugeot-do aniya.
ahmoogut-toe ahnee-yah.
아무것도 아니야.

**What are you
doing here?**

eojjeon iliya?
uh-chun illeeya?
어쩐 일이야?

—Nothing special.

geunyang.
geun-yahng.
그냥.

Really?

jeongmal?
chawng-mahl?
정말?

Are you serious?

jinjja?
jeen-jjah?
진짜?

Oh, yeah?

geurae?
geu-ray?
그래?

You're lying!

geojitmal!
guh-jeen-mahl!*
거짓말!

*The **t** sound in **geojitmal** becomes an **n** here (*guh-jeen-mahl*) when said in normal speech.

Are you lying?

geojitmaliji?
guh-jeen-mahlee-jee?
거짓말이지?

Don't lie!

geojitmal hajima!
guh-jeen-mahl hahjeemah!
거짓말 하지마!

Stop lying!

geojitmal geuman hae!
guh-jeen-mahl geumahn hay!
거짓말 하지 마! 그만 해!

What?

mwo?
mwo?
뭐?

Huh?

eoh?
aw?*
어?

*Said nasally, like the French **en**.

I don't believe it!

mideul su ga eopseo!
meed-eul soo gah upsaw!
믿을 수 가 없어!

Why?

wae?
way?
왜?

Why not?

wae aniya?
way ah-nee-yah?
왜 아니야?

You're joking!

nongdamiji!
nohng-dahmee-jee!
농담이지!

You're not joking?

nongdam aniji?
nohng-dahm ahnee-jee?
농담 아니지?

I'm not joking.

nongdam aniya.
nohng-dahm ahnee-yah.
농담 아니야.

He/She's joking!

nongdamiget-ji!
nohng-dahm-eeget-jjee!
농담이겠지!

Are you making fun of me?

nollinya?
nohllee-nyah?
놀리냐?

I guess so.

geureoket-ji.
geu-roh-get-jjee.
그렇겠지.

Maybe.

geureol keoya.
geurull ggoyah.
그럴 거야.

Maybe not.

anil keoya.
ah-neel kker-yah.
아닐 거야.

That's impossible!

maldo an dwae!
mahl-doe ahn dway!
말도 안 돼!

Dway or "day"—the **w** is almost not pronounced at all

You can't do that.

geureoken motae.
geu-roh-ken moat hay.
그렇겐 못 해.

I don't care.

sang-gwan eopseo.
sahng-gwahn upso.
상관 없어.

It's got nothing to do with me.

narang sang-gwan eopseo.
nah-rahng sahng-gwahn upso.
나랑 상관 없어.

I'm not interested.

gwansim eopseo.
gwahn-seem upso.
관심 없어.

I think that's it.

geugeoya.
geu-goyah.
그거야.

I think this is it.

igeoya.
ee-goyah.
이거야.

You're crazy!

neo micheo-sseo!
naw mee-chuss-o!
미쳤어!

Damn!

jegiral!
je-gee-rahl!
제기랄!

That's right.

maja.
mahj-ah.
맞아.

Is this it?

igeoya?
ee-goyah?
이거야?

This is it.

igeoya.
ee-goyah.
이거야.

Sure.

geureom.
geu-rum.
그럼.

It's true.

jinjjaya.
jeen-jjah-yah.
진짜야.

I understand.

alasseo.
ahlahsso.
알았어.

No problem. munje eopseo.
moonje upso.
문제 없어.

I like it! joa!
joe-ah!
좋아!

—Me, too. nado.
nahdoh.
나도.

OK! joa!
joe-ah!
좋아!

alasseo!*
ahlahsso!
알았어!

*Literally means "I know."

Hey! ya!
yah!
야!

Handle with care.

Great! joa!
joe-ah!
좋아!

Literally means "I like it."

I hope so. geureogil barae.
geuroh-kil bah-ray.
그러길 바래.

It's risky.	**wieomhae.** *wee-um hay.* 위험해.
Cheer up.	**him nae.** *heem nay.* 힘 내.
Smile.	**useo bwa.** *ooh-suh ba.* 웃어 봐.

2

Basic Phrases

Yes.	**ne.** (polite)
	nay.
	네.
	eung. (intimate)
	eung.
	응.
No.	**anio.** (polite)
	ahnee-oh.
	아니오.
	ani. (intimate)
	ahnee.
	아니.
Right.	**maja.**
	mahjah.
	맞아.
What?	**mwo?**
	mwo?
	뭐?

Who?	**nugu?** *noogoo?* 누구?
Where?	**eodi?** *uh-dee?* 어디?
When?	**eonje?** *on-jay?* 언제?
Why?	**wae?** *way?* 왜?
How?	**eotteoke?** *uh-tto-kay?* 어떻게?
Which?	**eotteon geo?** *uh-ttun go?* 어떤 거?
Whose?	**nugu kkeo?** *noogoo kko?* 누구 거?
This.	**igeo.** *eego.* 이거.
That.	**jeogeo.** (something over there) *juh-go.* 저거.

	geugeo. (something close to the listener)
	geugoh.
	그거.
Here.	**yeogi.**
	yohgee.
	여기.
There.	**jeogi.** (over there)
	johgee.
	저기.
	geogi. (close to the listener)
	gohgee.
	저기.
Maybe.	**geureol keoya.**
	geurull kkoya.
	그럴 거야.
Maybe not.	**anil keoya.**
	ahneel kkoya.
	아닐 거야.
I	**na**
	nah
	나
You	**neo**
	naw
	너
He/She	**jyae** (used in a person's presence, informal)
	jay
	쟤

gyae (used in a person's absence, informal)
gyay
걔

We

uri
ooree
우리

You (plural)

nedeul
nee-deul
네들

They

jyaenedeul (informal)
jyehne-deul
쟤네들

Don't!

haji ma!
hahjee mah!
하지 마!

Please.

jebal.
jebahl.
제발.

Thank you.

gamsahamnida (polite).
gahmsahm-needah.
감사합니다.

gomawo (intimate).
gohmahwah.
고마워.

Can I have this?

igeo gajeodo dwae? (informal)
eego gahjuh doe dway?
이거 가져도 돼?

How much is this?	**igeo eolmayeyo?** (polite)
	eego olmah-yay-yo?
	이거 얼마예요?
That's not cheap.	**ssan ge anieyo.** (polite)
	ssahn gay ahneeeyo.
	싼게 아니예요.
That's too expensive!	**neomu bissayo!** (polite)
	nuhmoo bee-sahyo!
	너무 비싸요!
I'm not buying this.	**igeo an sal kkeoyeyo.** (polite)
	eego ahn sahl kkoyay-yo.
	이거 안 살 거예요.
Make it cheaper and I'll buy it.	**jom deo ssa-myeon salkkeyo.** (polite)
	chohm duh ssahm-yuhn sahlkkay-yo.
	좀 더 싸면 살께요.

Haggling over prices happens mostly when you're buying something second-hand. There are still lots of open-air markets around, and a few of them are geared specifically toward tourists. There's still some room for haggling in places like this. But more and more shopping these days is done in large department stores, where the prices are fixed and marked—no haggling here.

For a shopping experience that combines traditional with modern, visit Namdaemun and Dongdaemun, two massive markets in Seoul. Dongdaemun is particularly famous for up-to-the-minute fashion, accessories and fabrics. Namdaemun is hundreds of years old, and boasts a lot of hard-to-find items. Both are great for a dose of Korean goods, food and people.

What are you looking for?	**mwo chaj-eu-se-yo?** *mwo chah-jeu-say-yo?* 뭐 찾으세요?
I'm just looking.	**Geu-nyang bo-neun geo-ye-yo.** *Geun-yang boh-neun goyay-yo.* 그냥 보는 거에요.
Don't worry.	**geok-jeong-ma-se-yo.** *kuck-juhng mah-say-yo.* 걱정마세요.
Here! (to call a salesperson)	**yeo-gi-yo!** *yo-gee-yo!* 여기요!
Do you have a bigger size?	**han chi-su keun geo iss-eo-yo?** *hahn chi-soo keun gaw issoyo?* 한 치수 큰 거 있어요?
Do you have a smaller size?	**han chi-su jak-eun geo iss-eo-yo?** *hahn chi-soo chahgeun gaw issoyo?* 한 치수 작은거 있어요?

Body language is common in Korea, just like in the West. This language has plenty of gestures of its own (and there are lots of websites that will show them to you, like Eat Your Kimchi (www.eatyourkimchi.com) and many others). Most Western gestures are OK (and if they're considered rude in the West, you might want to think twice about using them elsewhere).

Here are just a few useful tips.

- Give and receive with with both hands.
- When beckoning to an adult or hailing a cab, turn your palm downward (so different from the West) and wave your fingers toward you.
- All the chopstick rules you may have heard about in China or Japan apply in Korea, so don't point with chopsticks, don't stab food with them and don't leave them sticking up in your bowl of rice.
- If you ever feel inclined to play "got your nose" with a Korean child, don't. It's extremely offensive.

3

Got a Minute?

One moment.	**jamkkanmanyo.** *jahm-kkahn-mahn-yo.* 잠깐만요.
When?	**eonje?** *onjay?* 언제?
Till when?	**eonje kkaji?** *onjay kkahjee?* 언제까지?
What time?	**myeot-ssie?** *myawt-sshee?* 몇 시에?
Am I too early?	**na neomu iljjik wat-jji?** *nah nuhmoo eeljjeek waht-jjee?* 나 너무 일찍 왔지?
Is it too late?	**neomu neujeot-jji?** *nuhmoo neu-jut-jjee?* 너무 늦었지?

When is it good for you?

eonjega joa?
onjaygah joe-ah?
언제가 좋아?

What time is good for you?

myeot-ssiga joa?
myawt-sshee-gah joe-ah?
몇 시가 좋아?

How about later?

najung-e eottae?
nahjoong-ay ottay?
나중에 어때?

How about tomorrow?

naeil eottae?
nay-eel ottay?
내일 어때?

How about the day after tomorrow?

more eottae?
moray ottay?
모레 어때?

When can I come?

na eonje ohdo dwae?
nah onjay oh-doe dway?
나 언제 와도 돼?

When can we go?

uri eonje gal su isseo?
ooree onjay kahl soo isso?
우리 언제 갈 수 있어?

What time do we arrive?

uri myeot-ssie dochake?
*ooree myawt-shee-ay
  doe-chahk-hay?*
우리 몇 시에 도착해?

What time will we be back?

uri eonje jjeum dora wa?
ooree onjay-jjeum dohla wa?
우리 언제쯤 돌아와?

Are you ready?

junbi dwaesseo?
joonbee dwesso?
준비됐어?

When will you do it?

eonje hal keoya?
onjay hahl goyah?
언제 할 거야?

When will you be done?

eonje kkeutnael su isseo?
onjay kkeut-nel soo isso?
언제 끝낼 수 있어?

How long will it take?

eolmana geollyeo?
ullmahna kollyo?
얼마나 걸려?

—It'll be done soon.

geumbang dwoel keoya.
geum-bahng dwel kkoyah.
금방 될 거야.

Not now.

jigeumeun an dwae.
jeegeu-meun ahn dway.
지금은 안 돼.

Before.

geujeone.
geu-juh-nay.
그전에.

Next time.

da-eume.
dah-eum-ay.
다음에.

I don't know.

molla.
mohllah.
몰라.

I don't know when.   eonje iljji molla.
onjay eeljjee mohllah.
언제 일지 몰라.

I don't know now.   jigeumeun molla.
chihgeu-meun mohllah.
지금은 몰라.

I'm not sure.   hwakshilhi molla.
hwak-shilli mohllah.
확실히 몰라.

Any time's OK.   amuttaena joa.
ahmoo-ttay-nah joe-ah.
아무때나 좋아.

Every day.   maeil.
mail.
매일

You decide when.   niga eonjenji gyeoljjeonghae.
*neegah on-jen-jee gyull-juhng
    hay.*
네가 언젠지 결정해.

Whenever you want.   niga wonhaneun goseuro hae.
*neegah won-hahneun
    gohseuroh hay.*
네가 원하는 곳으로 해.

OK, let's meet then.   geureom, geuttae mannaja.
geurum, geuttay mahnnahjah.
그럼, 그때 만나자.

Let's go!   gaja!
gahjah!
가자!

Let's go for it.

han beon hae boja.
hahn bun hay pojah.
한 번 해 보자.

Hurry up.

ppalli ppalli.
ppahllee ppahllee.
빨리빨리.

Let's start again.

dasi haja.
dahshee hahjah.
다시 하자.

Let's continue.

gyesokaja.
gyesoh-kahjah.
계속하자.

I'll do it quickly.

ppalli halkke.
ppahllee hahl-kkay.
빨리 할께.

I'll finish soon.

geumbang kkeutnaelkke.
geum-bahng kkeut-nell-kkay.
금방 끝낼께.

Finished?

kkeutnasseo?
kkeunnasso?
끝났어?

—I'm finished.

kkeutnasseo.
kkeunnasso.
끝났어.

4

Hey There!

Listen to what I'm saying!	nae mal jom deuleobwa! *nay mahl chohm deul-uh-bwa!* 내 말 좀 들어봐!
Listen to him/her.	jyae mal jom deureobwa. *jyay mahl chohm deul-uh-bwa.* 쟤 말 좀 들어봐.
Listen to them.	jyaenedeul mal jom deureobwa. *jen-ay-deul mahl chohm deul-uh-bwa* 쟤네들 말 좀 들어봐.
Did you hear me?	nae mal deuleosseo? *nay mahl deulusso?* 내 말 들었어?
Can you hear me?	nae mal deullyeo? *nay mahl deullyaw?* 내 말 들려?

Literally means "Can you hear my voice clearly?"

Do you understand?
alasseo?
ahlahsso?
알았어?

Do you understand, or not?
arasseo, mollasseo?
ahlahsso, mohllasso?
알았어, 몰랐어?

Can you understand me?
nae mal iaehae?
nay mahl ee-hay-hay?
내 말 이해해?

—I don't understand.
iaega an dwae.
ee-haygah ahn dway.
이해가 안 돼.

I didn't understand.
jal mollasseo.
chahl mohlasso.
잘 몰랐어.

I couldn't understand.
iaehal su ga eopseosseo.
ee-hay-hal su ga upsusso.
이해할 수 가 없었어.

What?
mwo?
mwo?
뭐?

What did you say?
mworago haesseo?
mwo-ra-goh hesso?
뭐라고 했어?

I don't understand what you're saying.
museun malinji moreugesseo.
mooseun mahlinjee mohreugesso.
무슨 말인지 모르겠어.

Don't say such things.	**geureon mal haji ma.** *geuruhn mahl hahjee mah.* 그런 말 하지 마.
You shouldn't say things like that.	**geureon maleun hamyeon an dwae.** *geuruhn mahleun hamyuhn ahn dway.* 그런 말은 하면 안 돼.
Did you say that?	**nega geuraesseo?** *neegah geu-raysso?* 네가 그랬어?
You said that, right?	**nega geuraet-ji?** *neegah geureht-jjee?* 네가 그랬지?
I didn't say that.	**nan geureon mal han jeok eopseo.** *nahn geuruhn mahl hahn juck upso.* 난 그런 말 한 적 없어.
I didn't say anything.	**nan amumaldo an haesseo.** *nahn ahmoo-mahldoe ahn hesso.* 난 아무말도 안 했어.
I didn't tell anyone.	**amuhantedo mal an haesseo.** *ahmoo-hahntay-do mahl ahn hesso.* 아무한테도 말 안 했어.

Let's speak Korean!

han-gulmallo haja!
hahn-goong-mahllo hahjah!
한국말로 하자!

Literally means "Let's do it in Korean."

Can you speak Korean?

han-gukmal haseyo?
  (polite)
hahn-goong-mahl hahsay-yo?
한국말 하세요?

han-gukmal hae? (intimate)
hahn-goong-mahl hay?
한국말 해?

Please speak slowly.

cheoncheonhi malhae juseyo.
*chuhn-chuhn-hee mahlhay
  joo-say-oh.*
천천히 말해주세요.

How do you say this in Korean?

eo-ddeo-gae mal-hae-yo?
uh-ttoh-kay mahl-hay-yo?
어떻게 말해요?

Let's talk.

yaegi jom haja.
yay-gee chohm hahjah.
얘기 좀 하자.

Let's talk more.

jogeumman deo yaegihaja.
*chohmgeum-man duh yay-gee
hahjah.*
조금만 더 얘기하자.

Let's talk later.

ittaga yaegihaja.
eettah-gah yaygee-hahjah.
이따가 얘기하자.

Tell me later.

ittaga yaegihae jwo.
eettahgah yaygeehay jwo.
이따가 얘기해 줘.

I don't want to talk.

yaegihago sip-jji ana.
yaygee-hahgoh ship-jjee ahnah.
얘기하고 싶지 않아.

I don't want to talk with you.

neorang yaegi hago sip-jji ana.
naw-rahng yaygee hahgoh ship-jjee ahnah.
너랑 얘기하고 싶지 않아.

I don't want to hear about it.

geureon mal deud-ko ship-ji ana.
geuruhn mahl deud-kko ship-jji ahnah.
그런 말 듣고 싶지 않아.

I don't want to hear about that thing.

geu yaegin deud-ko ship-ji ana.
geu yaygeen deut-kko ship-jji ahnah.
그 얘긴 듣고 싶지 않아.

Don't make excuses!

byeonmyeonghaji ma!
byuhn-myuhng hahjee mah!
변명하지 마!

Don't give me no excuses!

pinggye ttawin deud-ko ship-ji ana!
ping-gyay ddah-win deud-kko ship-jji ahnah!
핑계 따윈 듣고 싶지 않아!

Stop complaining.

bulpyeong jom haji ma.

bool-pyuhng chohm hahjee mah.

불평 좀 하지 마.

Don't talk so loud.

neomu keuge malhaji ma.

nuhmoo kohge mahl-hahjee mah.

너무 크게 말하지 마.

Speak up.

keuge malhae bwa.

kohge mahlha bwah.

크게 말해 봐.

Speak louder.

deo keuge malhae bwa.

der kohge mahlha bwah.

더 크게 말해 봐.

Say it again.

dasi malhae bwa.

dahsee mahlha bwah.

다시 말해 봐.

Shut up.

sshiggeureoweo. (informal, but gentle)

sshee-ggeu-ruh-wa.

씨끄러워.

Shut up.

Dak chyeo. (really rude)

Dahk chaw!

닥쳐!

Talking loudly, particularly on public transportation, is bad form. Even though there's no taboo associated with taking or making a phone call while you're riding the subway, it's best to keep it short and quiet. If you talk too loudly, you just might earn yourself a *"Dak chyeo!"* (Another public transportation tip: stay off seats that are reserved for elderly people and pregnant women, even if there's no one around who's qualified to occupy them. It's considered disrespectful.)

5

Look at That!

Look at this!	igeo jom bwa! *eegull chohm bwah!* 이걸 좀 봐!
Don't look!	boji ma! *bojee mah!* 보지 마!
Don't look at this/that!	igeo/jeogeo boji ma! *eegull/juhgull bojee mah!* 이걸/저걸 보지 마!
Can you see it?	boyeo? *boyaw?* 보여?
—I can see it clearly.	jal boyeo. *chahl boyaw.* 잘 보여.
—I can't see it.	jal an boyeo. *chahl ahn boyaw.* 잘 안 보여.

Did you see that?

jeogeol bwasseo?
juhgull bwasso?
저걸 봤어?

Did you see it?

geugeol bwasseo?
geugull bwasso?
그걸 봤어?

—I saw it.

geugeol bwasseo.
geugull bwasso.
그걸 봤어.

—I didn't see it.

geugeol mot bwasseo.
geugull moat bwasso.
그걸 못 봤어.

I don't want to see it. bogo ship-ji ana.
bogo ship-jee ahnah.
보고 싶지 않아.

Did you see Jinju?

Jinjureul bwasseo?
jeenjooreul bwasso?
진주를 봤어?

I want to see you soon.

na neol ppalli bogoshipeo.
nah null ppahllee bogo ship-aw.
나 널 빨리 보고 싶어.

Are you going to meet Kim soon?

Kimeul got mannal keoya?
kimeul goad mannal goyah?
킴을 곧 만날 거야?

—I'm going to meet Kim soon.

Kimeul got mannal keoya.
Kimeul goad mannal goyah.
킴을 곧 만날 거야.

Did you meet John?   John mannasseo?
John mahn-nahsso?
존 만났어?

—I met John.   John mannasseo.
John mahn-nahsso.
존 만났어.

Well, we meet again.   eo, tto mannane.
uh, tto mahn-nah-nay.
어, 또 만나네.

6

Coming and Going

Come here!
iri wa!
eeree wah!
이리 와!

This is informal and mostly used when calling children.

Come later.
najung-e wa.
nahjoong-ay wah.
나중에 와.

Can you come?
ol su isseo?
ohl ssoo isso?
올 수 있어?

Come with me.
narang gachiga.
nah-rahng gah-cheegah.
나랑 같이 가.

He/She's coming here.
gyaen yeogi ol keoya.
gyen yogee ohl goyah.
걘 여기 올 거야.

They are coming here.

gyaenedeuleun yeogi ol keoya.
gyen-ay-deuleun yogee ohl goyah.
개네들은 여기 올 거야.

I'll go soon.

got gal keoya.
goad gahl goyah.
곧 갈 거야.

I'll come over soon.

got galke.
god gahlkkay.
곧 갈게.

I can go.

gal su isseo.
gahl ssoo isso.
갈 수 있어.

I think I can go.

gal su isseul geot gata.
gahl ssoo eesseul geot kah-ta.
갈 수 있을 것 같아.

I can't go.

mot-ka.
moat kka.
못 가.

I want to go.

na gago shipeo.
nah gahgo shipaw.
나 가고 싶어.

Do you want to go?

neo gago shipeo?
naw gahgo shipaw?
너 가고 싶어?

Do they want to go?

gyaenedeul gago shipeohae?
gyenay-deul gahgo shipuh-hay?
개네들 가고 싶어해?

I want to go to Seoul.	**na seoule gago shipeo.** *nah seoul-ay gahgo shipaw.* 나 서울에 가고 싶어.
I really want to go.	**na jeongmal gago shipeo.** *nah jerng-mahl gahga seeper.* 나 정말 가고 싶어.
I don't want to go.	**na gago ship-ji ana.** *nah gahgo ship-jji ahnah.* 나 가고 싶지 않아.
I really don't want to go.	**na jeongmal gago ship-ji ana.** *nah chongmahl gahgo ship-jji ana.* 나 정말 가고 싶지 않아.
You're going, right?	**neo gal keoji?** *naw gal gawji?* 너 갈 거지?
I'm going.	**na gal keoya.** *nah gahl goyah.* 나 갈 거야.
I'm not going.	**na an gal keoya.** *nah ahn gahl goyah.* 나 안 갈 거야.
I didn't go.	**na an gasseo.** *nah ahn gahsso.* 나 안 갔어.
Don't go!	**gaji ma!** *gahjee mah!* 가지 마!

Don't go yet!

ajik gaji ma!
ahjeek gahjee mah!
아직 가지 마!

I have to go.

na jigeum gaya dwae.
nah chigeum gahyah dway.
나 지금 가야 돼.

I really have to go now.

na jigeum kkok gaya dwae.
nah chigeum ggok gahyah dway.
나 지금 꼭 가야 돼.

May I go?

na gado dwae?
nah gahdo dway?
나 가도 돼?

I'm going/leaving.

na ganda.
nah gahndah.
나 간다.

Shall we go?

uri galkka?
ooree gahlkkah?
우리 갈까?

Let's go!

gaja!
gahjah!
가자!

Let's get outa here!

nagaja!
nah-gahjah!
나가자!

He/She left.

gyaen tteonasseo.
gyen ttuh-nasso.
걘 떠났어.

Stay here!

yeogi isseo!
yogee isso!
여기 있어!

**Where are you
    going?**

neo eodi ga?
naw uhdi ga?
너 어디 가?

Go slowly.

cheoncheoni ga.
chuhn-chuhn-hee ga.
천천히 가.

Eat, Drink, Be Merry!

I'm hungry.	**na baegopa.** *nah bay-go-pah.* 나 배고파.
I'm starving.	**baegopaseo juk.kesseo.** *bay-go-pah-suh chook-gesso.* 배고파서 죽겠어.

Literally means "I'm dying from hunger; I'm going crazy from hunger."

Have you eaten?	**neo bap meogeosseo?** *naw bahp mawgusso?* 너 밥 먹었어?

밥 (*bahp*) literally means "rice" but is often used in Korea to refer to any kind of meal.

—I haven't eaten yet.	**ajik an meogeosseo.** *ahjeek ahn maw-gusso.* 아직 안 먹었어.

Do you want to eat something?	mwo jom meogeullae? *mwo chohm mawg-eullay?* 뭐 좀 먹을래?
I'd like to eat something.	na mwo jom meok-kko shipeo. *nah mwo chohm maw-ko shipaw.* 나 뭐 좀 먹고 싶어.
Do you want some more?	deo meogeullae? *duh mawg-eullay?* 더 먹을래?
I'm thirsty.	na mokmalla. *nah mohng-mahllah.* 나 목말라.
I want to drink some beer.	na maekju mashigo shipeo. *nah meck-joo masheego shipaw.* 나 맥주 마시고 싶어.
I want some liquor.	na sul masigo shipeo. *nah sool masheego shipaw.* 나 술 마시고 싶어.
Try some ... (beverage)	... jom masyeo bwa. *... chohm mahsha bwa.* ... 좀 마셔 봐.
Korean vodka	soju *sohjoo* 소주
Mild, milky rice liquor	mak-keolli *mahk-gullee* 막걸리

Beer   **maek-ju**
meck-joo
맥주

Wine   **wain**
wa-een
와인

Plum wine   **maeshiljju**
maeshil-joo
매실주

Soju and beer   **somaek**
soh-meck
소맥

In Korea, soju and beer are often mixed together with a shot of soju poured into a glass of beer. This is called 소맥 (*soh-meck*), from the first syllables of each. Drink at your own risk.

Chicken and beer   **chimaek**
chee-meck
치맥

Fried chicken (치킨, *chee-geen*) and beer (맥주, *meck-joo*) go very well together and can be enjoyed together at fried chicken joints across Korea. This combination is called 치맥 (*chee-meck*) from the first syllables of each.

Hey, want to get some fried chicken and beer?   **Ya, chimaek meogeullae?**
Yah, chee-meck mawgeullay?
야, 치맥 먹을래?

This tastes too weird.   **mashi isanghae.**
mahshee eesahng-hay.
맛이 이상해.

I think this has gone bad.

igeo sang-han geot gata.
eego sahng-hahn gut gahta.
이거 상한 것 같아.

I think this stuff's stale.

igeo mashi gan geot gatae.
eego mahshee gahn gut gahta.
이거 맛이 간 것 같아.

Literally means "This taste has left."

Wow! This tastes good!

wa! mashitt-da!
wah! mahshit-ttah!
와! 맛있다.

More, more!

deo, deo!
duh, duh!
더, 더!

Do you want to drink some more?

deo mashillae?
duh mah-shillay?
더 마실래?

—Thank you, but I still have plenty.

ani, ajik mani namasseo.
*ahnee, ahjeek mahnee
nahm-ahsso.*
아니, 아직 많이 남았어.

Come on, dude, have some more!

geureoji malgo deo masyeo,
imma!
*geuruh-jee mahlgo duh
mahsha, eemmah!*
그러지 말고 더 마셔, 임마!

Handle the expression with care.

It's on me!

naega naelke!
naegah nell-kay!
내가 낼게!

Literally means "I'll pay!"

**Cheers! Salut!
Prost! Na zdravi!**

geon-bae!
gun-bay!
건배!

**Are you ready to
get wasted?**

juk-eul jun-bi dwaett-ni?
Jook-eul joon-bee dwet-nee?
죽을 준비됐니?

Literally, "Are you ready to die?"

**One shot / chug,
chug, chug!**

won-syat!
won-shot!
원샷!

**I'm not drunk.
(I'm sober)**

na an-chi-haess-eo.
nah ahn chee-hess-so.
나 안취했어.

I'm a little tipsy.

na jom eo-ji-reo-wo.
nah chohm aw-jee-raw-waw.
나 좀 어지러워.

I'm drunk.

na chi-haess-eo.
nah chee-hess-so.
나 취했어.

I feel like vomiting.

na to-hal geot ga-ta.
nah toe-hal goat gah-tah.
나 토할 것 같아.

I had a blackout.   pil-leum-ee
      ggeun-gyeo-sseo-yo.
pil-leum-ee ggeun-gyuss-oh-yo.
필름이 끊겼어요.

Literally means "film cut", the meaning is "I had a blackout" or "I blacked out." Picture the film getting cut, just like your memory getting cut after a few too many.

Hangover   suk-chwi
sook-chwee
숙취

Oh my God, this   A cham, i sukchwiga neomu
  hangover is awful.   apa.
Ah cham, ee sook-chwee-gah nuhmoo ah-pah.
아 참, 이 숙취가 너무 아파.

How about   bap meok-kko shipeo?
  some food?   *bahp mawg-ko shipaw?*
밥 먹고 싶어?

Is the food ready?   bap junbi da dwaesseo?
bahp joonbee dah dwesso?
밥 준비 다 됐어?

—Yeah, it's ready.   eung, da dwaesseo.
eung, dah dwesso.
응, 다 됐어.

Try this!   igeo jom meogeo bwa!
eego chohm mawgko bwah!
이거 좀 먹어 봐!

Try that!   jeogeo jom meogeo bwa!
juhgo chohm mawgko bwah!
저거 좀 먹어 봐!

Dude, stuff your face!

imma, ppalli meogeo!
eemmah, ppahl-lee mawgo!
임마, 빨리 먹어!

Handle the expression with care.

That looks delicious.

mashit-ketta.
mah-shee-get-dah.
맛있겠다.

Wow, it looks delicious!

wa, mashit-ketta!
wah, mah-shee-get-dah!
와, 맛있겠다!

Oh, that smells good!

ya, naemsae jota!
yah, namsa choh-tah!
야, 냄새 좋다!

What's this?

igeo mwoya?
eego mwoyah?
이거 뭐야?

Taste it.

mat jom bwa.
maht chohm bwah.
맛 좀 봐.

What's it called?

igeo ireumi mwoya?
eego eereumee mwoyah?
이거 이름이 뭐야?

Is it hot? (spicy)

maewo?
may-wa?
매워?

This is boiling!

tteugeowo!
tteu-guh-wa!
뜨거워!

Yuck!

eueuk!
eueuk!
으윽!

It tastes like shit!

mashi jiral gatae!
mahshee jeerahl gahta!
맛이 지랄 같아!

It's awful!

mat eopseo!
maht upso!
맛 없어!

I can't eat this!

mot meok-kesseo!
moan maw-gesso!
못 먹겠어!

Water, water!

mul, mul!
mool, mool!
물, 물!

My tongue's on fire!

ibeseo bul nanda!
eebesuh bool nahn-dah!
입에서 불난다!

Literally, "There's a fire in my mouth!"

How'd you eat this?

igeo eotteoke meogeo?
eego uh-ttoh-kay mawgo?
이거 어떻게 먹어?

Give me a fork.

pokeu jwo.
poh-keuh jwa.
포크 줘.

You want a knife?

kal julkka?
kahl jool-kkah?
칼 줄까?

Have some bulgogi.*   bulgogi jom meogeo bwa.
bool-go-gee chohm mawgo bwa.
불고기 좀 먹어 봐.

* Sweet and savory stir-fried beef.

I'd like to try some boshintang.*   na bosintang meogeo bogo shipeo.
nah boh-shin-thang mawgo bogo shipaw.
나 보신탕 먹어 보고 싶어.

* Dog-meat stew. Note that this is now eaten only rarely in Korea, and mainly by the older generation. This is not served at most restaurants—you need to find a specialty *boshintang* restaurant. There are still plenty of these around, but they are vastly outnumbered by just about every other kind of restaurant.

Careful, tteokbokki* is hot!   joshimhae, tteok-ppokkineun maewo!
joe-shim-hay, ttuck-pohk-ee-neun mae-wah!
조심해, 떡볶이는 매워!

* Rice cake mixed with hot chili paste.

That's a dip, don't drink it!   jeogeo meogneun geoya, mashiji ma!
juhgo muhngneun goyah, mahsheejee mah!
저거 먹는 거야, 마시지 마!

Give me some.   naege jom jwo.
nay-gay chohm jwa.
내게 좀 줘.

Give me a little more.   jogeum deo jwo.
choh-geum duh jwa.
조금 더 줘.

You want more food? deo meogeullae?
duh mawgeullay?
더 먹을래?

—I'd like more food. na deo meogeullae.
nah deo mawgeullay.
나 더 먹을래.

Enough? chungbunhae?
choong-boon-hay?
훙분해?

—Enough! chungbunhae.
choong-boon-hay.
훙분해.

I don't eat meat. na-neun go-gi-reul an
meo-geo.
na-neun go-gi-reul ahn mawgo.
나는 고기를 안 먹어.

Please make it less spicy. maeb-ji an-ge hae jwo.
mep-jee ahn-gay hay jwa.
맵지 않게 해 줘.

What is in this? yeo-gi-e mwo-ga
deul-eo-iss-eo?
yo-gee-ay mwo-gah deul-uh-isso?
여기에 뭐가 들어있어?

I can't eat ... ...mot meo-geo.
...mot mawgo.
… 못 먹어.

It's okay, I like spicy food.	**kwaenchanha, nan maeun eumshikeul chohahae.** *kwen-chahn-ah, nahn may-oon eumsheek-eul choh-ah-hay.* 괜찮아, 난 매운 음식을 좋아해.
I'm allergic to ...	**nan ... al-le-leu-gi-ga isseo.** *nahn ... ahl-leh-reu-gee-gah isso.* 난 … 알레르기가 있어
Milk	**oo-yoo** *oo-yoo* 우유
Eggs	**gye-ran** *gyay-rahn* 계란
Peanuts	**ddang-kong** *ddahng-kohng* 땅콩
Wheat	**mil** *mill* 밀
Gluten	**geul-lu-ten** *geul-loo-ten* 글루텐
Meat	**go-gi** *go-gee* 고기

I'm a vegetarian.   nan chae-shik-ju-ui-ja-i-ya.
nahn chay-sheek-joo-ee-jah
ee-yah.
난 채식주의자이야.

Note: Koreans tend not to understand this well and will consider chicken, fish, ham, or all sorts of other things as "not meat". Also, a lot of Korean food has seafood or other "hidden" meat in it. Kimchi, for example, is often made using anchovies. If you're very serious about your vegetarianism, you'll need to be very careful what you eat.

I don't eat meat.   go-gi an-meo-geo.
go-gee ahn-mawgo.
고기 안 먹어.

I don't eat meat   na-neun go-gi ha-go
or seafood.   hae-san-mul mot meo-geo.
nah-neun goh-gee hagoh
hay-sahn-mool moat mawgo.
나는 고기하고 해산물 못
먹어.

Korea has many types of restaurants. Street vendors are everywhere (though, at least in Seoul, they are technically illegal). They're very good for late-night after-drinking snacks. They're also good for snacking while drinking. Yes, you can get alcohol from some street vendors.

Among Korea's indoor restaurant options there are a lot of the Western chains (and other chains imitating the Western chains). These are pretty much exactly as you see them in the West, though they usually have a few regional menu items (e.g. the bulgogi burger, a hamburger with bulgogi sauce).

Korean fast-food places usually serve dishes like kimbap (rice, vegetables and some kind of meat rolled in seaweed) and noodles; these are good places to lunch, or to get a quick meal when you're eating alone.

Finally, there are large sit-down restaurants which usually have low tables and cushions for people to sit on the floor; they're designed with long tables for groups and in fact you usually must order at least two servings (Koreans prefer not to eat alone).

8

I Like It!

I like this.

na igeo mame deuleo.
 (objects)
nah eego mahmay deulaw.
나 이거 맘에 들어.

joa. (non objects)
joe-ah.
좋아.

I like that.

na jeogeo mame deuleo.
 (objects)
nah juhgo mahmay deulaw.
나 저거 맘에 들어.

joa. (non objects)
joe-ah.
좋아.

I really like that!

na geugeo jeongmal joa!
nah geugo chongmahl joe-ah!
나 그거 정말 좋아!

I don't like that.

na geugeo shileo.
nah geugo shillaw.
나 그거 싫어.

I don't really like it.

geugeo byeolloya.
geugo byulloh-ya.
그거 별로야.

No, thanks.

gwaenchanayo. (polite)
gwen-chahn-ahyo.
괜찮아요.

dwaesseoyo. (polite)
dwessoyo.
됐어요.

gwaenchana.
gwen-chahnah.
괜찮아.

dwaesseo.
dwesso.
됐어.

Gwaenchanayo and its more casual version **gwaenchana** mean "It's OK," while **dwaesseoyo** and the casual **dwaesseo** mean "It's done."

I want ...

na ... hallae.
nah ... hahllay.
나 ... 래.

This

igeo
eego
이거

That

jeogeo (something over there)
juhgo
저거

geugeo (something close to
the listener)
geugo
그거

I want ...
(used with nouns)

na ... gat-ko shipeo.
nah ... gaht-go shipaw.
나 ... 갖고 싶어.

I don't want ... a
(used with nouns)

na ... (gat-ki) sileo.
nah ... (gaht-gee) shillo.
나 ... (갖기) 싫어.

computer

keompyuteo
kuhm-pyoo-tuh
컴퓨터

camera

kamera
kahmerah
카메라

video recorder

bidio
beedeeo
비디오

TV

tibi
teebee
티비

CD

shidi
sheedee
시디

mobile phone

hyudaepon
hyoo-dae-pohn
휴대폰

laptop computer	noteubuk
	noh-teuh-book
	노트북
I don't need that.	na geugeo pilyo eopseo.
	nah geugo pill-yo upso.
	나 그거 필요없어.
I don't need this.	na igeo pilyo eopseo.
	nah eego pill-yo upso.
	나 이거 필요없어.

Note: you can leave out 나 (**na**) in most of the expressions below unless you need to clarify who you're talking about. It's more natural to leave it out, and people will usually assume you mean yourself unless the context makes this somehow unclear.

I'm busy.	na bappa.
	nah bahppah.
	나 바빠.
I'm happy.	na haengbokae.
	nah hayng-bohk-hay.
	나 행복해.
I feel good.	na gibun joa.
	nah gee-boon joe-ah.
	나 기분 좋아.
I'm glad to know that.	allyeo jwoseo gomawo.
	al-lyuh jwah-saw gomah-wah.
	알려줘서 고마워
I'm sad.	na seulpeo.
	nah seul-po.
	나 슬퍼.

I'm fine. na gwaenchana.
nah gwen-chahnah.
나 괜찮아.

I'm afraid. na museowo.
nah moo-saw-waw.
나 무서워.

I'm getting sick of it! jigyeowo!
jee-gyuh-wah!
지겨워.

I'm irritated! jjajeungna!
jjah-jeungnah!
짜증나!

Man, I'm irritated! ei, jjajeungna!
ayyy, jjah-jeungnah!
에이, 짜증나!

I'm confused! mwoga mwonji moreugesseo!
*mwogah mwonjee
    more-euh-gess-oh!*
뭐가 뭔지 모르겠어!

Literally means "I don't know which is which."

I'm going crazy. na michigesseo.
nah meechee-gesso.
나 미치겠어.

I'm losing my mind. na menbung sangtae-ya.
na men-boong sahng-tay-yah.
나 멘붕 상태야.

This is a relatively new slang term which is an abbreviation of another slang term, 멘탈 붕괴 (mental **bung-kwoe**). It literally means "mental breakdown," from the English "mental" and a Korean word for breakdown.

I'm pissed off!

na yeol badasseo!
nah yull bahdahss-oh!
나 열 받았어!

I'm mad! (angry)

na hwanasseo!
nah hwah-nahsso!
나 화났어!

I'm ready.

junbi da dwaesseo.
joon-bee dah dwesso.
준비 다 됐어.

I'm sleepy.

na jollyeo.
nah johl-lyaw.
나 졸려.

I'm tired.

na pigonhae.
nah pee-gohn-hay.
나 피곤해.

I'm wasted.

na kasseo.
nah kahssoh.
나 갔어.

Literally means "I left!" (too much alcohol, too many parties…)

I'm totally wasted!

na wanjeonhi gasseo!
nah wahn-juhn-hee gahssoh!
나 완전히갔어!

I'm out of it!

meoriga bingbing dora!
more-ee-ga bing-bing dohl-ah!
머리가 빙빙 돌아.

My head's going "ping!" i.e., it's spinning.

I'm bored!

shimshimhae!
shim-shim-hay!
심심해!

I feel sick.	**na apa.**
	nah ahpah.
	나 아파.
I'm disappointed.	**na shilmanghae.**
	nah shil-mahng-hay.
	나 실망해.
I'm disappointed in you.	**na neohante shilmanghae.**
	nah naw-hahn-tay shil-mahng-hay.
	나 너한테 실망해.
Oh, god! (How awful!)	**sesang-e!**
	say-sahng-ay!
	세상에!
What a pity!	**cham an dwaett-da!**
	chahm ahn dwet-dah!
	참 안 됐다!
Can you do it?	**neo hal su isseo?**
	naw hahl ssoo isso?
	너 할 수 있어?
—I can do it.	**na hal su isseo.**
	nah hahl ssoo isso.
	나 할 수 있어.
—I can't do it.	**na motae.**
	nah moat-hay.
	나 못 해.
Sorry, I can't do it.	**mianhajiman, an doegesseo.**
	meeahn-hahjee-mahn, ahn dway-gess-oh.
	미안하지만, 안 되겠어.

Sorry.

joesonghamnida. (polite)
chay-sawng-hahmneedah.
죄송합니다.

mianhae.
mee-ahn-hay.
미안해.

I can't believe it.

mideul suga eopseo.
meedeul ssoo gah upso.
믿을 수가 없어.

I'll do it.

naega halke.
nay-gah hal-kkay.
내가 할게.

I know.

algo isseo.
ahl-go Isso.
알고 있어.

I know him/her.

na jyae ala. (used in person's presence)
nah jyay ahl-aw.
나 쟤 알아.

na gyae ala. (used in person's absence)
nah gyay ahl-aw.
나 걔 알아.

Do you know that?

neo geugeo ara?
naw geugo ahl-aw?
너 그거 알아?

Oh, you know that.

neo geugeo aljana.
naw geugo ahl-jah-nah.
너 그거 알잖아.

I don't know.
na molla.
nah mohl-lah.
나 몰라.

I'll think about it.
jom saenggakhae bolke.
chohm sayng-kahk-hay bowl-kkay.
좀 생각해 볼게.

I'm so confused.
neomu het-kkallyeo.
nuhmoo het-kkahllyaw.
너무 헷갈려.

I made a mistake.
shilsuhaesseo.
shill-soo-hess-oh.
실수했어.

Am I right?
naega maja?
naygah mahjah?
내가 맞아?

Am I wrong?
naega teullyeo?
naygah teul-lyaw?
내가 틀려?

9

Curses and Insults

What do you want?	**mwoya?** *mwoyah?* 뭐야?
What do you want, asshole?	**mwoya, imma?** *mwoyah, eemmah?* 뭐야, 임마?
What?	**mwo?** *mwo?* 뭐?
What you lookin' at?	**mwol bwa?** *mwol bwah?* 뭘 봐?
Anything wrong?	**kkomnya?** *kkohm-nyah?* 꼽냐?

You givin' me attitude?

eojju, jjaeryeo bwa?
uh-jjoo, jjay-ryuh bwah?
어쭈, 째려 봐?

Literally means "Why are you looking down on me?"

What are you staring at?

mwol cheoda bwa?
mwol chuhdah bwah?
뭘 쳐다 봐?

—None of your business.

namiya.
nahm-eeyah.
남이야.

Literally means "Other person." The idea is: "That is the kind of question you could ask yourself, but I'm not you—so it's none of your business!"

Mind your own business.

chamgyeonhaji ma.
chahm-gyuhn-hahjee mah.
참견하지 마.

Go away!

kkeojeo!
gguh-jaw!
꺼져!

Go away, man!

kkeojeo, imma!
gguh-jaw, eemmah!
꺼져, 임마!

What a moron!

meong-cheong-ee sae-ggi!
muhng-chuhng-ee sae-ggi!
멍청이 새끼!

Fuck off!

jot-kka!
joht-kkah!
좆까!

Literally means "Kick penis!" From **jot**, "penis," and **kka**, "kick."

What did you just say?

banggeum mworago haesseo?

bahng-geum mwo-rahgo hessoh?

방금 뭐라고 했어?

Do you know who I am?

naega nugunjina ala?

naygah noogoon-jeenah ahlah?

내가 누군지나 알아?

Come here, I'll teach you some manners!

ssagaji eopsneun saekkiya, iri wa!

ssah-gahjee awm-neun sekkee-ya, eeree wah!

싸가지 없는 새끼야, 이리 와!

Literally means "You have no manners, you baby; come here!"

Come here!

iri wa!

eerree wah!

이리 와!

Don't joke with me!

nongdamhaji ma!

nohng-dahm-hahjee mah!

농담하지 마!

Stop it!

geuman hae!

geu-mahn hay!

그만 해!

Shut up!

ip dakcheo!

eep dahkchaw!

입 닥쳐!

What're you doing?

mwo haneun jishiya?

mwo hah-neun jee-sheeyah?

뭐 하는 짓이야?

What'd you hit me for?

wae cheo?
way chaw?
왜 쳐?

What'd you push me for?

wae mileo?
way meelaw?
왜 밀어?

I'm gonna kill you!

neo jugyeo beoril keoya!
naw joogyaw boh-rill goyah!
너 죽여 버릴 거야!

Want to die?

chukillae?
chook-uhl-lay?
죽을래?

Have you finished?

da kkeutnasseo?
dah kkeun-nahssoh?
다 끝났어?

You wanna fight?

mat-jjang tteo?
maht-jjahng ttaw?
맞장 떠?

We gonna fight, or not?

ssaul keoya, mal keoya?
ssah-ool goyah, mahl goyah?
싸울 거야, 말 거야?

Let's fight and see!

han beon hae bojagu!
hahn buhn hay boh-jah-goo!
한 번 해 보자구!

Ouch!

aya!
ahyah!
아야!

Don't!

geuman!
geu-mahn!
그만!

That hurts!

apa!
ahpah!
아파!

Help!

sallyeo juseyo!
sallyuh joo-say-oh!
살려 주세요!

dowajuseyo!
doh-wah-jooseyo!
도와주세요!

Don't hit me!

ttaeriji ma!
ttay-reejee mah!
때리지 마!

You deserve it!

majado ssa!
mahj-ahdoh ssah!
맞아도 싸!

Don't do it again!

dashin hajima!
dah-sheen hah-jeemah!
다신 하지마!

Say you're sorry!

sagwahae!
sahgwah-hay!
사과해!

—Sorry.

mianhae.
mee-ahnhay.
미안해.

You're right.
niga maja.
neegah mahjah.
네가 맞아.

Though 네가 (you) looks like it should be pronounced "*nay-gah*," it's almost always pronounced "*neegah*" to distinguish it from 내가 (I).

I was wrong.
naega teullyeosseo.
naygah teul-lyuhss-oh.
내가 틀렸어.

It was my fault.
naega jalmotaesseo.
naygah chahl-moat-hess-oh.
내가 잘못했어.

Forgive me.
yongseohae jwo.
yong-suh-hay jwaw.
용서해 줘.

I forgive you.
yongseohae julkke.
yong-suh-hay joolkkay.
용서해 줄게.

**You're making
me laugh!**
ut-kkine!
oot-kkeenay!
웃기네!

You win.
niga igyeosseo.
neegah ee-gyuss-oh.
네가 이겼어.

I lose.
naega jeosseo.
naygah juss-oh.
내가 졌어.

SPECIAL KOREAN INSULTS

Fugly

mae-ju
may-joo
매주

Literally "fermented beans," this means a freakin' ugly person.

Gold digger

dwen-jang-nyeo
dwen-jang-nyaw
된장녀

Literally, "bean paste girl"—the implication here is that they're superficial and shallow—this person can't tell shit from bean paste.

Retard / moron
(stone head)

dol-dae-geo-ri
dol-day-gaw-ri
돌대가리

No common sense / idiot

gae-nyeom-eops-da
gay-nyuhm-awp-da
개념없다

개념 is derived from a Korean word meaning "notion," and is commonly used to mean "common sense." 없다 means "to not exist," so you can see why this would be offensive.

You're lower than an insect.

beollemando motan saekki.
bawl-lay-mahn-doe moat-hahn say-kkee.
벌레만도 못한 새끼.

Son of a beggar.

geoji saekki.
guhjee sekkee.
거지 새끼.

Son of a bitch.

gae saekki.
gay sekkee.
개 새끼.

Son of an idiot.

babo saekki.
bahboh sekkee.
바보 새끼.

Fuck!

sshibal!
ssheebahl!
씨발!

Note: to censor yourself, say 아이씨 *"ah-ee-shi"*—it's like saying "aw-ffff"—like you're going to say it but then don't.

Fuck you!

sshibal nom! (to male)
sshee-bahl nohm!
씨발 놈!

sshibal nyeon! (to female)
sshee-bahl nyuhn!
씨발 년!

sshibangsae!
sshee-bahngsay!
씨방새!

You peasant!

ssyangnyeon! (women)
sshang-nyuhn!
쌍년!

ssyangnom! (men)
sshang-nohm!
쌍놈!

You look like a penis!

jot-kateun nom! (men)
joat-kkahteun nohm!
좃 같은 놈!

jot-kkateun nyeon! (women)
joat-kkahteun nyuhn!
좃 같은 년!

You piece of shit!
jot-tto anin saekki!
joat-doe ahneen sekkee!
좆도 아닌 새끼!

In contrast to the above expression, this one literally means "You're not even a penis"—as in, you're not even worth calling a dick.

Don't show off!
jalnan cheok hajima!
chahllahn chuck hahjee-mah!
잘난 척 하지마!

Go drink your mother's breast milk and then come back!
gaseo eomma jeojina deo meok-kko wa!
gahsaw um-mah juhj-eenah duh mawk-go wah!
가서 엄마 젖이나 더 먹고 와!

Go home and masturbate!
jibe gaseo ttalttalina cheo!
jeebay gahsoh ttahl-ttahl-eenah chaw!
집에 가서 딸딸이나 쳐!

Are you insane?
neo byeongshiniya?
naw byuhng-shin-ee-ya?
너 병신이야?

Crazy man!
michin nom!
mee-cheen nohm!
미친 놈!

Crazy woman!
michin nyeon!
mee-cheen nyuhn!
미친 년!

Note: This one is actually really bad, so don't say it unless you're 100% certain you mean it and really want to anger someone.

Ah, stupid!

ah, meongcheong-han saekki!
*ahh, muhng-chuhng-hahn
  sekkee!*
아, 멍청한 새끼!

Dickhead!

dolttaegari!
dohltta-gahree!
돌대가리!

Pig!

jijeobunhan saekki!
jeejuh-boonhahn sekkee!
지저분한 새끼!

Bad-luck-woman!

jaesu eopsneun nyeon!
jaysoo uhm-neun nyuhn!
재수 없는 년!

Bad-luck-man!

jaesu eopsneun saekki!
jaysoo um-neun sekkee!
재수 없는 새끼!

**Oh, I lost my
    appetite!**

ah, bapmat eopseo!
ahh, bahm-maht upso!
아, 밥 맛 없어!

Implies that the person being insulted is so unseemly that the speaker's stomach is turning.

Pervert!

byeontae saekki!
byuhntay sekkee!
변태 새끼!

Oh, shit smell!

ah, neojeobunhan saekki!
*ahh, nuh-juh-boon-hahn
  sekkee!*
아, 저분한 새끼!

Die!

dwejeo beoryeo!
dwejuh borryaw!
뒈져 버려!

Why don't you go somewhere and die!

eodi gaseo dwejeo beoryeo!
uhdee gah-suh dwejuh borryaw!
어디 가서 뒈져 버려!

What a fucking mess!

ah, sshipal jot-kkanne!
ahh, ssheep-ahl joat-kkahn-ne!
아, 씹할 좆 같네!

You motherfucker!

nimi sshipal nom!
neemee ssheep-ahl nohm!
니미 씹할 놈!

Bitch!

gae gateun nyeon!
gay gaht-eun nyuhn!
개 같은 년!

10

Party Talk

All the expressions in this section are polite speech.

Do you come here often?	yeogi jaju oseyo? *yogee jahjoo oh-say-oh?* 여기 자주 오세요?
You look like you're having fun.	cham jaemi isseo boineyo. *chahm jem-ee eessuh boh-ee-nay-yo.* 참 재미 있어 보이네요.
—Yes, I'm having fun.	ne, jaemi isseoyo. *nay, jay-mee iss-uh-yo.* 네, 재미 있어요.
This is fun!	**shinnanda** *shin-nahn-dah* 신난다

A Casanova,
a sweet talker

je-bi
jay-bee
제비

This guy is out to suck up or sweet talk in order to get laid. If you hear this, take this as a sign that things aren't going well.

This place is
happening!

yeogi kwaenchanta!
yogee quench-ahntah!
여기 괜찮다!

Note that 괜찮다 (**kwaenchanta**) literally means "okay", so if you say this phrase but don't sound excited, you'll be taken to mean, "This place is just okay."

—Yeah, this place is
happening!

ye, yeogi kwaenchanayo!
ye, yogee quench-ahn-ahyo!
예, 여기 괜찮아요!

This place is fun!

yeogi jeongmal jaemisseoyo!
yogee chong-mahl
  jay-mee-iss-uh-yo!
여기 정말 재밌어요!

This place is
fantastic!

yeogi meosisseoyo!
yogee mush-iss-uh-yo!
여기 멋있어요!

What's your name?

ireumi eotteoke dwoeseyo?
eereum-ee uh-ttoh-kay
  dwess-say-yo?
이름이 어떻게 되세요?

—My name is ...

je ireumeun ... ieyo.
jay ee-reum-eun ...ee-ay-yo.
제 이름은 ... 이에요.

Are you here alone?	**honja wasseoyo?** *hohn-jah wahss-uh-yo?* 혼자 왔어요?
—Yes, I'm here alone.	**ne, honja wasseoyo.** *nay, hohnjah wahss-uh-yo.* 네, 혼자 왔어요.
—No, I'm here with my …	**anio, … rang wasseoyo.** *ahnee-oh … rahng wahss-uh-yo.* 아니오, … 랑 왔어요.
Older sister	**eonni** (female) *uhnnee* 언니 **nuna** (male) *noonah* 누나
Older brother	**oppa** (female) *oh-ppah* 오빠 **hyeong** (male) *hyuhng* 형
Younger sister/ brother	**dongsaeng** *dohng-seng* 동생
Friends	**chin-gu** *chin-goo* 친구

Boyfriend

namjachin-gu
nahm-jah-chin-goo
남자친구

Girlfriend

yeojachin-gu
yoh-jah-chin-goo
여자친구

Husband

nampyeon
nahm-pyuhn
남편

Wife

anae
ah-nay
아내

Senior

seonbae
sun-bay
선배

Junior

hubae
hoobay
후배

Gay

geh-ee
geh-ee
게이

Lesbian

lae-jeu-bi-an
lae-jew-bee-ahn
레즈비안

Transgendered
seong-jeon-hwan-ja
sawng-jawn-hwan-ja
성전환자

When trying to ask someone if they're gay or lesbian, you may not want to draw attention to it. In the Western world, one might ask "Which way do you swing?" or "Are you family?" Try 이쪽이세요? (*i-jjok-i-sae-yo*) to ask the same kind of indirect question in Korean—literally, it's "are you this way?" or "are you this direction?"

Can I join you?
hap-seokhaedo doelkkayo?
*hahp-ssuck-hay-doh
   dwel-kkahyo?*
합석해도 될까요?

Can I sit here?
yeogi anjado doelkkayo?
yogee ahnjah-doh dwel-kkahyo?
여기 앉아도 될까요?

Please sit down.
ye, anjeuseyo.
yay, ahnjeu-say-yo.
예, 앉으세요.

**Is someone sitting
   here?**
yeogi nugu isseoyo?
yogee noogoo issuh-yo?
여기 누구 있어요?

**—Someone's sitting
here.**
yeogi nugu isseoyo.
yogee noogoo issuh-yo.
여기 누구 있어요.

**Can I buy you
   a drink?**
sul han jan sado doelkkayo?
*sool hahn jahn sahdoh
   dwel-kkahyo?*
술 한 잔 사도 될까요?

Where are you from?	**eodiseo wasseoyo?**
	awdww-suh wah-ssuh-yo?
	어디서 왔어요?
—I'm from …	**jeoneun … eseo wasseoyo.**
	jaw-neun … ay-suh
	wah-ssuh-yo.
	저는 … 에서 왔어요.
the U.S.	**miguk**
	mee-gook
	미국
England	**yeongguk**
	young-gook
	영국
France	**peurangseu**
	peurang-seu
	프랑스
Australia	**hoju**
	hohjoo
	호주
Germany	**dogil**
	doh-gill
	독일
Canada	**kaenada**
	kennah-dah
	캐나다
Italy	**itallia**
	eetahl-leeah
	이탈리아

Russia	**reoshia** *rawsheea* 러시아
Korea	**han-guk** *hahn-gook* 한국
Japan	**il-bon** *eel-bohn* 일본
China	**jungguk** *joong-gook* 중국
Hong Kong	**hongkong** *hohng-kohng* 홍콩
Indonesia	**indoneshia** *eendoh-neh-sheeah* 인도네시아
Thailand	**taeguk** *taygook* 태국
Where do you live?	**eodie salayo?** *uh-di sahl-ahyo?* 어디에 살아요?
—**I live in ...**	**... e salayo.** *... ay sahlahyo.* ... 에 살아요.

New York	**nyuyok**
	nyuyohk
	뉴욕
L.A.	**elei**
	el eh-ee
	엘에이
Seoul	**seo-ul**
	suh-ool
	서울
Busan	**busan**
	boo-sahn
	부산
London	**reondeon**
	ruhn-duhn
	런던
Sydney	**shideuni**
	shee-deunee
	시드니
Melbourne	**melbeon**
	melbuhn
	멜번
Paris	**pari**
	pahree
	파리
Rome	**roma**
	rohmah
	로마

How old are you?	**naiga eotteoke doeseyo?**
	nah-eegah uh-ttuh-kay
	dwesay-yo?
	나이가 어떻게 되세요?
—I'm ... years old.	**... salieyo.**
	... sahlee-eyo.
	... 살이에요.
15	**yeol daseot**
	yull dahsuht
	열다섯
16	**yeol yeoseot**
	yull yull-suht
	열여섯
17	**yeol ilgop**
	yull eel-gohp
	열일곱
18	**yeol yeodeol**
	yull yuh-dull
	열여덟
19	**yeo aop**
	yull ahohp
	열아홉
20	**seumul**
	seu-mool
	스물
21	**seumul han**
	seu-mool hahn
	스물한

22 **seumul dul**
seu-mool dool
스물둘

23 **seumul set**
seu-mool set
스물셋

24 **seumul net**
seu-mool net
스물넷

25 **seumul daseot**
seu-mool dahsuht
스물다섯

26 **seumul yeoseot**
seu-mool yawsuht
스물여섯

27 **seumul ilgop**
seu-mool eelgohp
스물일곱

28 **seumul yeodeol**
seu-mool yuh-dull
스물여덟

29 **seuml aop**
seu-mool ahawp
스물아홉

30 **seoreun**
saw-reun
서른

31	**seoreun hana** *saw-reun hahna* 서른하나
32	**seoreun dul** *saw-reun dool* 서른둘
33	**seoreun set** *saw-reun set* 서른셋
34	**seoreu net** *ser-roh net* 서른넷
35	**seoreun daseot** *saw-reun dahsuht* 서른다섯
40	**ma-heun** *mah-eun* 마흔
50	**swin** *sween* 쉰
Are you a student?	**hak-saeng-iseyo?** *hahk-sseng-eesay-yo?* 학생이세요?
I'm a ...	**jeoneun ... ieyo.** *jaw-neun ... ee-yay-yo.* 저는 ... 이에요.

Doctor

uisa
wee-sah
의사

Dentist

chikkwa uisa
chee-kkwah wee-sah
치과의사

Lawyer

byeonhosa
byuhn-ho-sah
변호사

Professor

gyosu
gyohsoo
교수

Secretary

biseo
beesuh
비서

Teacher

gyosa
gyoh-sah
교사

Nurse

ganhosa
gahn-hoh-sah
간호사

Business person

sa-eopkka
sah-upkkah
사업가

Company employee

hoesawon
hway-sahwawn
회사원

Public servant

gongmuwon
gohng-moo-wawn
공무원

Hairdresser

miyongsa
mee-yong-sah
미용사

Sales person

yeong-eop sawon
young-up sah-wawn
영업사원

What kinds of hobbies do you have?

chwimiga eotteoke doeseyo?
chwee-meegah uh-ttuh-kay dwesay-yo?
취미가 어떻게 되세요?

—My hobby is ...

je chwimineun ... ieyo.
jay chwi-meeneun ... ee-ay-yo.
제 취미는 ... 이에요.

Sport

undong
oon-dohng
운동

Tennis

teniseu
ten-nee-seu

Golf

golpeu
goal-peu
골프

Music

eumak
eu-mahk
음악

Cooking	**yori** *yoree* 요리
Fishing	**nak-sshi** *nahk-sshee* 낚시
Skiing	**seuki** *seukee* 스키
What music do you like?	**eotteon eumakeul joahaeyo?** *aw-ttuhn eu-mahk-eul choe-ah-hay-yo?* 어떤 음악을 좋아해요?
—I like ...	**jeoneun ... joahaeyo.** *jawneun ... choe-wah-hayo.* 저는 ... 좋아해요.
Do you like (Gangnam Style)?	**(Gangnam seutaileul) joahaeyo?** *(Gangnam seu-tah-ill)eul joe-ah-hay-yo?* (강남스타일) 좋아해요?
Yes, I do the horse dance very well.	**ne, jeon malchum chal haeyo.** *nay, jawn mahl-choom chahl hay-yo.* 네, 전 말춤을 잘 해요.
Let's see it.	**geureom boyeoyo.** *geu-ruhm boy-uh-joe-yo.* 그럼 보여줘요.

No, I hate it.	anio, chongmal shilheoyo.
	ah-nee-oh, chong-mahl shill-uh-yo.
	아니요, 정말 싫어요.
You know this song?	i norae alayo?
	ee noh-ray ahlahyo?
	이 노래 알아요?
—Yes, I do.	ne, alayo.
	nay, ahlahyo.
	네, 알아요.
—I don't know it.	jal mollayo.
	chahl mohl-lahyo.
	잘 몰라요.
—This is the first time I'm hearing it.	cheo-eum deuleoyo.
	chaw-eum deul-uh-yo.
	처음 들어요.
Would you like to dance?	chum chullaeyo?
	choom choollay-yo?
	춤 출래요?
—I can't dance.	chum mot chwoyo.
	choom moat chwoyo.
	춤 못 춰요.
—I'm not in the mood.	chum chul gibuni anieyo.
	choom chool geeboon-ee ahnee-ay-yo.
	춤 출 기분이 아니에요.
You dance well.	chum jal chuneyo.
	choom chahl choonay-yo.
	춤 잘 추네요.

Shall we go elsewhere?

eodi dareun dero gallaeyo?
uh-di dah-reun day-roh gahl-lay-yo?
어디 다른 데로 갈래요?

What time do you have to be home?

myeot-shikkaji jibe gaya dwaeyo?
myawt-sshee-kkah-jee jeep-ay gahya dway-yo?
몇 시까지 집에 가야 돼요?

What time are you leaving?

myeot-shie gal keoyeyo?
myawt-sshee-ay gahl ggoy-ay-yo?
몇 시에 갈 거예요?

—I have to go now.

jigeum gaya dwaeyo.
jee-geum gahyah dway-yo.
지금 가야 돼요.

Don't go now.

jigeum gaji maseyo.
jee-geum gahjee mahsay-yo.
지금 가지 마세요.

Go later!

ittaga gaseyo!
eettahgah gah-say-yo!
이따가 가세요!

What shall we do?

mwo hallaeyo?
mwo hahllay-yo?
뭐 할까요?

What's next?

ije mwo halkkayo?
eejay mwo hahl-kkahyo?
이제 뭐 할까요?

—It's up to you.

hago shipeun daero haseyo.

*hahgoh sheepeun day-roh
   hah-say-yo.*

하고 싶은 대로 하세요.

**Do you wanna come
   to my place?**

uri jibeuro gallaeyo?

ooree jeeb-eur-roh gahl-lay-yo?

우리 집으로 갈래요?

—I'm not sure.

jal moreuge-sseoyo.

chahl moh-reu-gess-oh-yo.

잘 모르겠어요.

Just for coffee.

geunyang keopi mashireo
   gayo.

*geu-nyahng kaw-pee
   mah-shee-ruh gahyo.*

그냥 커피 마시러 가요.

—Yes, let's go.

ne, galleyo.

ne, gah-lay-yo.

네, 갈래요.

11

Getting Serious

I want to know more about you.	neo-e dae-aeseo deo algo shipeo. *naw-ay day-hay-saw duh ahlgo ship-aw.* 너에 대해서 더 알고 싶어.
Shall we meet again?	uri tto mannalkka? *ooree ttoh mahn-nahl-kkah?* 우리 또 만날까?
When can I see you again?	eonje dashi mannal su isseo? *onjay dahshee mahn-nahl ssoo isso?* 언제 다시 만날 수 있어?
Can I call you?	naega jeonwahaedo dwae? *naygah juhnwah-haydoh dway?* 내가 전화해도 돼?
Will you call me?	nahante jeonwahallae? *nah-hahnay juhwah-hahllay?* 나한테 전화할래?

Here's my phone number.	**igeo nae jeonwabeonoya.**
	eego nay juhnwah-buhn-ho-yah.
	이거 내 전화번호야.
What's your number?	**jeonwabeonoga etteoke dwae?**
	juhnwah-buhn-ho-gah uh-ttuh-kay dway?
	전화번호가 어떻게 돼?
—My phone number is ...	**nae jeonwabeononeun ...**
	nay juhnwah-buhn-ho-neun...
	내 전화번호는 ...
563 – 4718	**o-yuk-sam (e) sa-chil-il-pal**
	oh-yook-sahm (e) sah-cheel-eel-pahl
	오육삼 (에) 사칠일팔
890 – 1234	**pal-gu-gong. (e) il-i-sam-sa**
	pahl-goo-gohng (e) eel-ee-sahm-sah
	팔구공 (에) 일이삼사

1 il	**2** i	**3** sam	**4** sa	**5** o
일 *eel*	이 *ee*	삼 *sahm*	사 *sah*	오 *oh*

6 yuk	**7** chil	**8** pal	**9** g	**0** gong
육 *yook*	칠 *cheel*	팔 *pahl*	구 *goo*	공 *gohng*

What's your e-mail address?	**imeil jusoga eotteoke dwae?**
	eemay-eel joo-soh-gah uh-ttuh-kay dway?
	이메일 주소가 어떻게 돼?

— **My e-mail address is ...**

nae imeil jusoneun ... ya.
nay ee-may-il joo-soh-neun... ya.
내 이메일 주소는 ... 야.

It was fun.

jaemi isseosseo.
jaymee eess-uss-oh.
재미 있었어.

*See Chapter 13

12

On the Phone

Hello.	**yeoboseyo.** *yoh-boh-say-yo.* 여보세요.
Hi, Mary? **This is Robert.**	**annyeong haseyo, Mary-** **iseyo? Jeon Robert-indeyo.** (polite) *ahnyoung hahsay-oh,* *Mary-ee-say-oh? Jon* *Robert-in-day-oh.* 안녕하세요, 메리이세요? 전 로버트인데요.

Wait a minute.

jamkkanman gidariseyo.
  (polite)
jahm-kkahn-mahn
  gee-dah-reessay-yo.
잠깐만 기다리 세요.

It's me, Robert.

na Robeoteuya.
nah Raw-berteu-yah.
나 로버트야.

What are you doing?

jigeum mwo hae?
jee-geum mwo hay?
지금 뭐 해?

Shall we meet now?

jigeum mannalkka?
jee-geum mahn-nahl-kkah?
지금 만날까?

I wanna see you.

na neo bogo shipeo.
nah naw boh-goh ship-aw.
나 너 보고 싶어.

I can't go out now.

jigeum motnaga.
jee-geum moan-nahgah.
지금 못 나가.

I'll call you tomorrow.

naega naeil jeonwahalkke.
nay-gah nay-ill
  chuhn-wah-hahl-kkay.
내가 내일 전화할게.

Bye!

jal isseo!
chahl isso!
잘 있어.

Literally means "Stay well" usually said by the person who called.

—Yes.

eung, geurae!
eung, geu-ray!
응, 그래！

Excuse, me, could you please put your phone on vibrate mode?

Shillyehajiman hokshi handeuponeul jindongmodeuro haenoha juseyo. (polite)
Shill-lay-hah-jee-mahn hoak-shee handeu-pone-eul jin-dohng-moh-deu-ro hay-noh-ah joo-say-yo.
실례하지만 혹시 핸드폰을 진동모드로 해놓아 주세요.

Sure, sorry.

Ne, choesonghamnida. (polite)
Nay, chway-sohng-hahm-nee-dah.
네, 죄송합니다.

I'd rather not.

choesonghajiman andwoegesseoyo. (polite)
chway-sohng-hah-jee-mahn ahn-dway-gess-uh-yo.
죄송하지만 안되겠어요.

I'm expecting an important call.

Jeoneun jungyohan cheonhwareul kidarigo isseoyo. (polite)
Jaw-neun joong-yoh-hahn chuhn-wah-reul kee-dah-ree-goh iss-uh-yo.
저는 중요한 전화를 기다리고 있어요.

You're breaking up.

chal an deullyeo.
chahl ahn deul-lyuh.
잘 안 들려.

This actually translates "I can't hear you."

I hear you.

deullyeo.
deul-lyuh.
들려.

(For more phrases on hearing see chapter 4)

My battery is low.

bateori chungjeon eolma an namasseo.
bah-tuh-ree choong-juhn ohlmah ahn nah-mahss-aw.
배터리 충전이 얼마 안 남았어.

Reception is bad here.

yeogi sushini an dwae.
yoh-gee soo-shin-ee ahn dway.
여기에 수신이 안 돼.

Do you mind if I take this?

cheonhwa badado dwae?
chuhn-wah bah-dah-doe dway?
전화를 받아도 돼?

Cell phones are even more ubiquitous in Korea than in the West, and have been for some time. Everyone has a smart phone.

While many western cultures consider it rude to make/take calls or texts while you're with someone, or have public phone conversations, Koreans (particularly the younger generation) don't have a big problem with it.

Phones are allowed at school but usually the teacher will collect them all in a basket at the beginning of the school day and give them back at the end so students won't use them during class.

It's illegal to use a cell phone while driving, but people seem to do it anyway.

Why are you always taking so many selfies?
Wae gyesok selka hae?

Because I'm a really beautiful person.
Nan cheongmal yeppeun saramieoseo.

Why did you unfriend me?
Neon wae nawa chingureul ggeungyeosseo?

Because your updates are boring.
Ne eopdeiteuneun jaemieopseoseo.

13

On the Computer

If you're using a Korean computer, you'll have to put up with a couple more buttons on the keyboard and a lot more Korean on your screen. While you can probably navigate a computer based on the icons alone, it's nice to have a bit of vocabulary as well!

Start	**shi-jak**
	shee-jahk
	시작

Just like the Windows "Start" button.

My Computer	**nae keom-pyu-teo**
	nay kom-pyoo-taw
	내컴퓨터

My Documents	**nae mun-seo**
	nay moon-saw
	내 문서

Internet

in-teo-net
een-teo-net
인터넷

My Pictures

nae geu-rim
nae geu-rim
내그림

Recycle Bin

hyu-ji-tong
hyu-jee-tohng
휴지통

Notepad

me-mo-jang
meh-moh-jang
메모장

E-mail

jeon-ja me-il
jeon-ja may-il
전자 메일

Literally, "Electronic Mail." On most websites, e-mail is simply
이메일 **ee-may-il** or even 메일 (**me-il**).

Control Panel

je-eo-pan
jay-aw-pahn
제어판

**Network / Network
   Connections**

ne-teu-wo-keu
neh-teu-wuh-keu
네트워크

Run...

shil-haeng
shil-hayng
실행

Calculator

gye-san-gi
gyay-sahn-gi
계산기

Confirmation hwak-in
hwahk-in
확인

You might see this Korean on the computer screen wherever you might see 'OK' if it were in English.

IN WINDOWS EXPLORER

File pa-il
pah-ill
파일

Edit pyeon-jib
pyeon-jeep
편집

View bo-gi
boh-gee
보기

Tools do-gu
doe-goo
도구

Help do-oom-mal
doe-oom-mahl
도움말

Search geom-saek
guhm-seck
검색

Music eum-ak
eum-mahk
음악

Video	**bi-di-o**
	bee-dee-oh
	비디오

Add 내, or **nay**, in front of these to say 'My Music' or 'My Photos'.

IN INTERNET EXPLORER/WORD/ HANGEUL WORD PROCESSOR

New tab	**sae taep**
	say tap
	새 탭

New window	**sae chang**
	say chang
	새 창

Open	**yeol-gi**
	yawl-gee
	열기

Save	**jeo-jang**
	jaw-jahng
	저장

Save As...	**da-reun-i-reum-eu-ro jeo-jang**
	da-reun-ee-reum-eu-ro jaw-jang
	다른이름으로 저장

Print	**in-swae**
	in-sway
	인쇄

Print Preview	**in-swae-mi-ri-bo-gi**
	in-sway-mee-ree-bo-gee
	인쇄미리보기
Cut	**jal-la-nae-gi**
	jal-lah-nay-gee
	잘라내기
Copy	**bok-sa**
	bohk-sah
	복사
Paste	boot-yeo-neo-gi
	boot-yaw-naw-gee
	붙여넣기

GREAT, SO HOW DO I TYPE IN KOREAN?

On Korean keyboards, there's a button to the right of the space bar marked 한/영 (**han/yeong**—the first syllables of Korean and English in the local language, respectively). As you might have guessed, hitting this will toggle between Korean letters and English letters.

Send me a...	**nal ... reul pone jweo.**
	nal ... reul poh-nay jwa.
	날 ⋯ 를 보내 줘.
I'll send you a...	**nega ...reul ponelge.**
	nay-gah ...reul poh-nel-gay.
	내가 ⋯를 보낼게.

Text message

munja
moon-jah
문자

Facebook message

peiseu-buk meshiji
paiseu-book mesh-ih-jee
페이스북 메시지

Email

imeil
ee-may-ill
이메일

Often abbreviated to just 메일 (*may-ill*)

Kakaotalk message

Kakaotok meshiji
Kah-cow-toke mesh-ih-jee
카카오톡 메시지

Update

eopdeiteu
uhp-deh-ee-teu
업데이트

News Feed

nyuseupideu
nyoo-seu-pee-deu
뉴스피드

Messages

meshiji
mesh-ih-jee
메시지

Events

ibenteu
ee-ben-teu
이벤트

Post

gyeshi
gyeh-shee
계시

Like	**joayo** *joe-ah-yo* 좋아요
Leave a comment	**daetgeul dalgi** *deht-geul dahl-gee* 댓글 달기
Share	**gongyuhagi** *gohng-yoo-hah-gee* 공유하기
Tweet	**teuwit** *teu-weet* 트윗
Follower	**pallowo** *pall-loe-wuh* 팔로워
Connect	**chinhaejigi** *chin-hay-jee-gee* 친해지기
Discover	**balgyeonhagi** *bahl-gyuhn-hah-gee* 발견하기
Tag	**taegeu** *tay-geu* 태그
Hashtag	**haeshitaegeu** *hash-ee-tay-geu* 해시태그

Do you have a ... account?	**neo ... gyejeong isseo?** *naw... gyay-juhng isso?* 넌 … 계정 있어?
Kakaotalk	**kakaotok** *kah-cow-toke* 카카오톡

Often shortened to just 카톡 (*ka-toke*)

Facebook	**peiseubuk** *peh-ee-seu-book* 페이스북
Twitter	**teuwiteo** *teu-wee-tuh* 트위터

Note that while Koreans are familiar with Facebook and Twitter, they aren't yet widely used within Korea, with most Koreans preferring to use native Korean social networking sites. At the time of this writing these include Cyworld (싸이월드, "*ssa-ee-wool-deu*"), Me2Day (미투데이, "*Mee-too-deh-ee*," which is usually just written in English anyway) and the messaging program Kakaotalk (카카오톡, "*kah-cow-toke*"). The first two are essentially blogging sites (think Tumblr) while Kakaotalk is a free instant messaging app that is also available in English.

I have to update my...	**naega ...reul eopdeiteu halge.** *nay-gah ...reul uhp-deh-ee-teu halkkay.* 내가 …를 업데이트 할게.
I'm going to post this on Facebook/Twitter.	**igeol ...e ollilge.** *ee-gull ...ay ohl-lill-kkay.* 이걸 …에 올릴게.

Hey, don't put this on Facebook/ Twitter!

ya, igeol …e ollijima!

ya, ee-gull …ay ohl-lee-jee-mah!

야, 이걸 …에 올리지마!

Like my post/page.

nae (gyeshimul/peiji/sajin) eul joahae.

nay (gyay-shee-mool/ peh-ee-jee/sah-jin)eul joe-ah-hay.

내 (계시물/페이지/사진)을 좋아해.

Why haven't you liked my post yet??

wae ajik nae (gyeshimul/peiji/ sajin)eul an joahaesseo?

way ah-jeek nay (gyay-shee-mool/peh-ee-jee/sah-jin)eul ahn joe-ah-hess-oh?

왜 아직 내 (계시물/ 페이지/사진)을 안 좋아했어?

I unfriended (him/her/you).

(geu/geunyeo/neo) chingu ggeunhgyeosseo.

(geu/geu-nyaw/naw) chin-goo ggeun-kkyuss-oh.

(그/그녀/너) 친구 끊겼어.

Did you see what John posted?

neo joni mweol ollyeotneunji bwasseo?

naw john-ee mwull ohl-lyuht-neun-jee bwah-ssoh?

너 존이 뭘 올렸는지 봤어?

Tag me in that photo.

geu sajine nal taegeuhae.
geu sah-jin-ay nahl tay-geu-hay.
그 사진에 날 태그해.

Don't tag me in that photo!

geu sajine nal taegeuhajima!
geu sah-jin-ay nahl tay-geu-hah-jee-mah!
그 사진에 날 태그하지마!

Let's be friends on...

uri ...ro chingu haja.
ooree ...roh chin-goo hahjah.
우리 …로 친구 하자.

Yeah, add me.

ne, haja.
eung, hahjah
응, 하자.

I'd rather not.

mami an deuleo.
mahm-ee ahn deul-aw.
맘이 안 들어.

Send me a friend request.

nal chingu yocheongeul bonae jweo.
nahl chin-goo yoh-chuhng-eul boh-nay jwaw.
날 친구 요청을 보내 줘.

What's your username?

ne sayongja ireumi mwoya?
nee sah-yohng-jah ee-reum-ee mwoh-ya?
네 사용자 이름이 뭐야?

It's...

ireumi ...ya.
ee-reum-ee ...yah.
이름이… 야.

Do you have a website/blog?

neon (hompeiji/beullogeu) isseo?

nawn (hoam-peh-ee-jee/ beul-loh-geu) isso?

넌 (홈페이지/블로그) 있어?

Yes, my website/ blog address is...

ne, (hompeiji/beullogeu) neun ...ya.

nay, (hoam-peh-ee-jee/ beul-loh-geu)neum ...yah.

응, (홈페이지/블로그)는 …야.

No, I don't.

ani, eopseo.

ah-nee, uhp-so.

아니, 없어.

Could you write down your username for me?

ne (sayongja ireumeul/ hompeijireul/ beullogeureul) jom jeokeo jwo.

nee (sah-yohng-jah ee-reum-eul/ hoam-peh-ee-jee-reul/beul-loh-geu-reul) chohm juck-uh jwaw.

네 (사용자 이름을/ 홈페이지를/블로그를) 좀 적어 줘.

I can't see you. What are your privacy settings?

neol mot bwa. ne gonggae
    beomwi seoljeongi eottae?
*null moat bwah. nee gohng-gay
    buhm-wee sull-juhng-ee
    aw-ttay?*
널 못 봐. 네 공개 범위
    설정이 어때?

Friends only

chingumaniya
chin-goo-mahn-ee-yah
친구만이야

Public

jeonche gonggaeya
juhn-chay gohng-gay-yah
전체 공개야

Are you friends with …?

neon …kwa chinguya?
nawn …kwah chin-goo-yah?
넌 …과 친구야?

Why did you unfriend me?

neon wae nawa chingureul
    ggeungyeosseo?
*nawn way nah-wah chin-goo-
    reul kkeun-kyuss-oh?*
넌 왜 나와 친구를 끊겼어?

Because I don't like you anymore.

neol chigeum shilheoseo.
null chee-geum shill-uss-aw.
널 지금 싫어서.

Because you update too often.

neomu jaju eopdeiteuhaeseo.
*nawmoo jah-joo uhp-deh-ee-
    teu-hay-saw.*
너무 자주 업데이트해서.

Because you never update.

eopdeiteu byeollo an haeseo.
uhp-deh-ee-teu byull-oh ahn hay-saw.
업데이트 별로 안 해서.

Because your updates are boring.

ne eopdeiteuneun jaemieopseoseo.
nee uhp-deh-ee-teu-neun jay-mee-uhp-saw-saw.
네 업데이트는 재미없어서.

Your Facebook profile says you're (married/in a relationship).

ne peiseubuk gyejeonge euihae neon (gihon/yeonae jung)iya.
nee peh-ee-seu-book gyay-juhng-ay eu-ee-hay nawn (gee-hohn/yuhn-ay joong) eeyah.
네 페이스북 계정에 의해 넌 (기혼/연애 중)이야.

I lied.

geuge geojitmaliya.
geugay guh-jit-mahl-ee-yah.
그게 거짓말이야.

It's not serious.

jungyohaji anha.
joong-yoh-hah-jee ahn-ah.
중요하지 않아.

Oh, she's/he's just a friend.

(geu/geunyeo)neun chingumaniya.
(geu/geu-nyaw)neun chin-goo-mahn-ee-yah.
(그/그녀)는 친구만이야.

I just put that to get my parents off my back.

nae bumonimi gyesok
     jollaseo geureohke haesseo.
nay poo-moh-neem-ee gyay-
     soak johl-lass-aw geu-roh-kay
     hess-oh.
내 부모님이 계속 졸라서
     그렇게 했어.

It's complicated.

bokjaphan gwangyeya.
boak-jahp-hahn gwahn-gyay-
     yah.
복잡한 관계야.

Do you play ...?

neon ...reul hae?
nawn ...reul hay?

Let's play together.

kati haja.
kah-chi hah-jah.
같이 하자.

Sure.

ne, haja.
eung, hah-jah.
응, 하자.

I'd rather not.

shilheo.
shill-aw.
싫어.

Selfie

selka
sell-kah
셀카

Why are you always taking so many selfies?

wae gyesok selka hae?
way gyay-soak sell-kah hay?
계속 셀카 해?

Because I want to show my ...what I'm doing.

nae ...mwol hago itneunji boyeogo shipeoseo.

nay ... ay-gay- mwoll hah-go it-neun-jee boh-yuh-ju-go ship-aw-saw.

내 ...에게 뭘하고 있는지 보여주고 싶어서.

Friends

chingu

chin-goo

친구

Family

kajok

kah-joak

가족

Mother

eomma

uhm-mah

엄마

Father

appa

ah-ppah

아빠

Boyfriend

namjachingu

nahm-jah-chin-goo

남자친구

Girlfriend

yeojachingu

yaw-jah-chin-goo

여자친구

Husband

nampyeon

nahm-pyuhn

남편

Wife	anae
	ah-nay
	아내

Because I'm a really ... person.	nan cheongmal ... saramieoseo.
	nahn chong-mahl ...sah-rahm-ee-aw-saw.
	난 정말 … 사람이어서.

Handsome	jal saengin
	chahl sayng-in
	잘생긴

Beautiful	yeppeun
	yep-eun
	예쁜

Vain	heuiddeun
	hee-dduh-oon
	희떠운

TEXTING

Note: as with English slang, Korean text-talk goes out of date really quickly. However, the expressions below have all been around for at least a few years and show some staying power.

~ makes your sentence sound friendlier; no exact English equivalent, but sort of like a smiley

☺ **I like you**   chohahae
choh-ah-hay
좋아해~

^^ smiley face :)

☺ **I like you**   chohahae
                       choh-ah-hay
                       좋아해^^

ㅠㅠ sad face (meant to look like tears streaming down from the eyes)

☹ **I have to go now**   nan chigeum kaya dwae
                       nahn chigeum kay-yah dway
                       난 지금 가야 돼 ㅠㅠ

ㅎㅎ, ㅋㅋ both represent laughter (think **lol** or **hehehe**). The more letters, the more laughter.

That was so funny!   Cham utkyeo!
  LOL!   *Cham oot-kyaw!*
                       참 웃겨 ㅎㅎ
                       참 웃겨 ㅋㅋ

ㅇㅇ indicates agreement—an abbreviation of 응 (**eung**), which means "yeah".

"That was so funny,   "Cham utkiji kkk" "Eung"
  right?" "Yeah!"   *"Cham oot-keejee kkk" "Eung"*
                       "참웃기지 ㅋㅋㅋ" "ㅇㅇ"

; indicates embarrassment—the more semicolons, the more embarrassment

I failed my test;;;   Naega shiheome
                         ddeoleojyeosseo ;;;
                       Nay-gah shee-um-ay ddull-uh-
                         jyuhsso.
                       내가 시험에 떨어졌어 ;;;

헐, 헉 expressions of astonishment, sort of like "Whoa!" or "Wow!" Not just used in texting, but in speech as well.

Wow! You failed the test?
Heol/heok! Shiheome ddeoleojyeosseo?
Hull/huck! Shee-um-ay ddull-uh-jyuhsso?
헐! 시험에 떨어졌어?

짱 the best, the greatest. Not just used in texting, but in speech as well.

Girls' Generation rock!
Sonyeo shidaeneun jjangida!
Soh-nyuh shee-day-neun jjahng-ee-dah!
소녀시대는 짱이다!

꽝 the worst, a total failure. Not just used in texting, but in speech as well.

That date sucked.
Geu deiteuneun ggwangieosseo.
Geu deh-ee-teu-neun ggwahng-ee-uhsso.
그 데이트는 꽝이었어.

You can also add ㅁ, ㅇ to the end of your sentences while texting; this makes them sound "cute". They often follow the 요 at the end of a polite sentence, and can follow other vowels at the end of words as well.

I know.
Alasseoyong./Alasseoyom.
ahlassoyong./Ahlassoyom.
알았어용.

You busy?	**Neo chigeum bappang?/ bappam?**
	Naw chigeum bappahng?/ bappahm?
	너 지금 바빰?

Similarly, 네 (yes, "*nay*") is often written as 넵 ("*nep*") to sound cute.

14

Lover's Language

I love you.
saranghae.
sahrahng-hay.
사랑해.

I'm crazy about you.
nan neoga joa michigesseo.
nahn nawgah joe-ah meechee-gessoh.
난 너가 좋아 미치겠어.

I'm yours.
nan nikeoya.
nahn nee-kkoy-ya.
난 니꺼야.

You're mine.
neon naekeoya.
nawn nay-kkoy-ya.
넌 내꺼야.

You're beautiful.
neo cham yeppeo. (to women)
naw chahm yeppaw.
너 참 예뻐.

You're handsome.
neo cham jal saenggyeosseo.
(to men)
naw chahm chahl sayng-gyuss-oh.
너 참 잘 생겼어.

You're sexy.
neo sek-ssihae.
naw sek-sshee-hay.
너 섹시해.

Your ... is/are beautiful.
neo ... yeppeo.
naw ... yeppaw.
너 ... 예뻐.

Eyes
nun
noon
눈

Lips
ip-ssul
eep-ssool
입술

Hands
son
sohn
손

Face
eolgul
ull-gool
얼굴

Legs
dari
dahree
다리

Nose
ko
koh
코

Breasts

gaseum
gahseum
가슴

Neck

mok
mohk
목

Shoulder

eokkae
uh-ggay
어깨

Butt

eongdeong-i
ohng-derng-ee
엉덩이

**You have a
  beautiful body.**

neon mommae-ga yeppeo.
nawn mohm-may-gah yeppaw.
넌 몸매가 예뻐.

You smell nice.

neohanten jo-eun naemsaega
  na.
*naw-hahn-ten joe-eun nehm-
  say-gah nah.*
너 한텐 좋은 냄새가 나.

Can I kiss you?

kiseuhaedo dwae?
keeseuh-haydoe dway?
키스해도 돼?

Kiss me!

kiseuhae jwo!
kee-seuh hay jwah!
키스해 줘!

**Do you wanna sleep
  with me?**

narang jago shipeo?
  nah-rahng chah-goh ship-aw?
나랑 자고 싶어?

Oh, I'm embarrassed.   ai, changpihae.
ahee, chahng-pee-hay.
아이, 창피해.

Don't be shy.   bukkeureowo haji ma.
boo-kkeu-ruh-wah hahjee mah.
부끄러워 하지 마.

Close your eyes.   nun gama bwa.
noon gahmah bwah.
눈 감아 봐.

Turn off the light.   bulkkeo bwa.
bool-kkuh bwah.
불꺼 봐.

IN THE BEDROOM

Is this your first time? *neo cheo-eumiya?*
naw chuh-eumeeyah?
너 처음이야?

Tell me the truth.   sashildaero malhae bwa.
sahsheel-dayroh mahlhay bwah.
사실대로 말해 봐.

I'm still a virgin.   na ajik cheonyeoya. (female)
nah ahjeek chuhn-yuh-yah.
나 아직 처녀야.

na ajik chonggagiya. (male)
nah ahjeek chohng-gahk-ee-yah.
나 아직 총각이야.

I'm frightened.

museowo.
moo-suh-wah.
무서워.

Don't worry.

geok-jjeonghaji ma.
guck-juhng-hah-jee mah.
걱정하지 마.

I'll be careful.

joshimhalke.
joe-shim-hahl-kkay.
조심할게.

I wanna hold your hand.

neo sonjaba bogo shipeo.
naw sohn jah-pah boh-goh ship-aw.
너 손 잡아 보고 싶어.

Look into my eyes.

nae nun cheoda bwa.
nay noon chuh-dah bwah.
내 눈 쳐다 봐.

Hug me.

na ana jwo.
nah ahn-ah jwaw.
나 안아 줘.

Take your ... off!

... beoseo bwa!
... buss-uh bwah!
... 벗어 봐!

Clothes

ot
oat
옷

Jeans

cheongbaji
chuhng-bahjee
청바지

Dress
deureseu
deu-resseuh
드레스

Skirt
chima
cheemah
치마

T-shirt
tisyeocheu
tee-shut-cheu
티셔츠

Socks
yangmal
yahng-mahl
양말

Sneakers
shinbal
sheen-bahl
신발

Shoes
kudu
koodoo
구두

Bra
beura
beurah
브라

Underwear
paenti
pen-tee
팬티

The Korean word **paenti**, despite its derivation from the English "panty," is gender-neutral.

I'm cold!
na chuwo!
nah choowaw!
나 추워!

Make me warm.

ttatteutage hae jwo.
ttahtteut-hahgay hay jwaw.
따뜻하게 해 줘.

Come closer to me.

deo gakkai wa.
duh gah-kka-ee wah.
더 가까이 와.

That tickles.

ganjireowo.
gahnjee-ruh-wah.
간지러워.

IN BED

**I wanna see
  your ...**

na ni ... bogo shipeo.
nah nee ... boh-goh ship-aw.
나 니 ... 보고 싶어.

**I wanna touch
  your ...**

na ni ... manjigo shipeo.
*nah nee ... mahn-jeegoh
  ship-aw.*
나 니 ... 만지고 싶어.

**I wanna suck
  your ...**

na ni ... ppalgo shipeo.
nah nee ... ppahl-goh ship-aw.
나 니 ... 빨고 싶어.

Thing

kkeo
kkaw
거

Breasts

gaseum
gahseum
가슴

Pussy	**boji** (derogatory form)
	bohjee
	보지
	geogi (gender neutral)*
	guh-gee
	거기
Dick	**jaji** (derogatory form)
	jahjee
	자지
	geogi (gender neutral)*
	guh-gee
	거기

* **Geogi** literally means "there."

Balls	**bul-al**
	bool-ahl
	불알
Nipples	**jeot-kkok-jji**
	juht-kkoak-jjee
	젖꼭지
Butt	**eongdeong-i**
	uhng-duhng-ee
	엉덩이
Knees	**mureup**
	moo-reup
	무릎
Toes	**balkarak**
	bahl-kahrahk
	발가락

Fingers

sonkarak
sohn-kahrahk
손가락

**I'm afraid I'll get
pregnant.**

imshinhalkka bwa museowo.
*eem-sheen-hahl-kkah bwah
moo-suh-wah.*
임신할까 봐 무서워.

Use a condom!

kondom sseo!
kawn-dawm ssaw!
콘돔 써!

**I don't like to wear
a condom.**

kondom sseuneun ge shilheo.
*kawn-dawn sseu-neun gay
shil-aw.*
콘돔 쓰는 게 싫어.

**If you don't wear
a condom,
I won't do it!**

kondom an sseumyeon, an
halkeoya!
*kawn-dawm ahn sseu-myuhn
ahn hahl-goy-yah!*
콘돔 안 쓰면, 안 할꺼야!

Oh, it feels so good!

ah, gibun joa!
ahh, geeboon joe-ah!
아, 기분 좋아!

Touch me!

na manjeo jwo!
nah mahnjuh jwaw!
나 만져 줘!

Bite me!

kkaemuleo jwo!
kkay-mool-uh jwaw!
깨물어 줘!

More, more!

jogeumman deo, jogeumman
  deo!
*joe-geum-mahn duh,
  joe-geum-mahn duh!*
조금만 더, 조금만 더!

Deeper, deeper!

deo gipi, deo gipi!
duh geepee, duh geepee!
더 깊이, 더 깊이!

Faster, faster

deo ppalli, deo ppalli!
duh ppahllee, duh ppahllee!
더 빨리, 더 빨리!

Harder, harder!

deo sege, deo sege!
duh say-gay, duh say-gay!
더 세게, 더 세게!

Wait, wait!

jamkkanman, jamkkanman!
*jahm-kkahn-mahn, jahm-
  kkahn-mahn!*
잠깐만, 잠깐만!

**I'm coming,
  I'm coming!**

naonda, naonda! (men)
nah-ohndah, nah-ohndah!
나온다, 나온다!

oreul kkeo gatae! (women)
oh-reul kkuh gah-tay!
오를 거 같아!

I came.

na ssasseo. (men)
nah ssahssaw.
나 쌌어.

na ollasseo. (women)
nah ohl-lass-uh.
나 올랐어.

—**I know.**

ala.
ahlah.
알아.

Did it feel good?

gibun joasseo?
gee-boon joe-ah-sso?
기분이 좋았어?

Let's get married.

uri kyeolhonhaja.
ooree kyull-hoan-hah-jah.
우리 결혼하자.

**I wanna be
your wife.**

ni anaega doego shipeo.
*nee ahnaygah dway-goh
ship-aw.*
네 아내가 되고 싶어.

**I wanna be
your husband.**

ni nampyeoni doego shipeo.
*nee nahm-pyawnee dway-goh
ship-aw.*
네 남편이 되고 싶어.

**I don't want to get
married yet.**

ajigeun gyeolhonhago
shipji anha.
*ahjeegeun kyull-hoan-hah-goh
ship-jee-ahn-ah.*
아직은 결혼하고 싶지 않아.

I'm too young.

jigeumeun neomu illeo.
jee-geum-eun nuh-moo ill-uh.
지금은 너무 일러.

Literally means "It's too early."

I'm already married.

na gyeolhonhaesseo.
nah gyull-hoan hess-oh.
나 결혼했어.

**I love you, but
I can't become
your wife/husband.**

neol saranghajiman, ne
   anaeneun/nampyeoneun
   doel su eopseo.
*null sah-rahng-hah-jee-mahn,
   nee ah-nay-neun/nahm-
   pyuhn-eun dwell ssoo upso.*
넬 사랑하지만, 네 아내 는/
   남편은될 수 없어.

I need time to think.

saenggakhal shigani pilyohae.
*sayng-gahk-hahl shee-gahn-ee
   pill-yo-hay.*
생각할 시간이 요해.

This is so sudden.

neomu gap-jjagiya.
nuhmoo gahp-jjah-gee-yah.
무 갑자기야.

**We must think
about this.**

uri deo saenggakhae bwaya
   doel keo gatae.
*ooree duh sayng-gahk-hay
   bwah-yah dwell kkuh gah-tay.*
우리 더 생각해 봐야 될 거
   같아.

**Do you want to
come to ...
with me?**

narang ... gallae?
nahrahng ... gahllay?
나랑 ... 갈래?

the USA

miguk
meegook
미국

Canada

kaenada
kanahdah
캐나다

Europe	**yureop**
	yooruhp
	유럽
Australia	**hoju**
	hohjoo
	호주
I want to stay in Korea.	**na hanguge itko shipeo.**
	nah hahn-goo-gay eet-kkoh ship-aw.
	나 한국에 있고 싶어.

15

Farewell

Let's not see each other again.	**uri dashineun mannaji malja.** *ooree dah-sheeneun mahn-nahjee mahljah.* 우리 다시는 만나지 말자.
I hate you!	**neol shileo!** *null shillaw!* 널 싫어!
Don't call me again.	**dashin jeonwahaji ma.** *dah-sheen chuhnwah-hahjee mah.* 다신 전화하지 마.
Get lost!	**kkeojeo!** *kkuh-jaw!* 꺼져!
Give it up, already.	**pogihae.** *poh-gee-hay.* 포기해.

I don't love you anymore.

deo isang neol saranghaji ana.
duh ee-sahng null sah-rahng-hah-jee ahn-ah.
더 이상 널 사랑하지 않아.

You're boring.

neo jaemi eopseo.
naw jeh-mee upso.
재미없어.

Literally means "You're no fun."

Stop following me.

gwichanke gulji ma.
gwee-chahnkay gooljee mah.
귀찮게 굴지 마.

Do you have another lover?

dareun sarami saenggyeosseo?
dahreun sah-rahm-ee sayng-gyuss-oh?
다른 사람이 생겼어?

It's my fault.

naega jalmotaesseo.
naygah chahl-moat-hessoh.
내가 잘못했어.

Can we start again?

dashi shijak hal sun eopseo?
dahshee sheejahk hahl soon upso?
다시 시작할 순 없어?

I can't live without you.

neo eopshin sal su eopseo.
naw up-sheen sahl ssoo upso.
너 없인 살 수 없어.

Please understand me.

jebal na jom ihaehae jwo.
jaybahl nah chohm ee-hay-hay jwaw.
제발 나 좀 이해해 줘.

I'll never forget you.

neol ijeul sun eopseul keoya.
nerl ee-jeul soon upseul goy-yah.
널 잊을 순 없을 거야.

Can we still be friends?

uri chin-guro jinael su isseo?
ooree cheen-gooroh jee-nell soo isso?
우리 친구로 지낼 수 있어?

I'll always love you.

neol eonjena saranghal keoya.
null awn-jehn-ah sah-rahng-hahl goy-yah.
널 언제나 사랑할 거야.

I'll miss you.

bogo shipeo jil keoya.
bohgoh ship-aw-jill goy-yah.
보고 싶어질 거야.

I'll always think about you.

eonjena neo saenggak halke.
onjaynah naw sayng-gahk hahl-kkay.
언제나 너 생각할게.

I'll call you when I come back.

dolawaseo jeonhwa halke.
dohl-uh-wah-suh chuhn-wah hal-kkay.
돌아와서 전화할게.

I'll be back soon.

got olke.
goat ohl-kkay.
곧 올게.

Do you have to go?

ggok gaya dwae?
ggohk gahyah dway?
꼭 가야 돼?

Please don't go!

jebal gaji ma!
jaybahl gahjee mah!
제발 가지 마!

Stay here with me.

narang gachi yeogi isseo.
nah-rahng gahch-ee yogee isso.
나랑 같이 여기 있어.

I have to go.

na gaya dwae.
nah gahyah dway.
나 가야 돼.

Try to understand.

ihaehae jwo.
ee-hay-hay jwaw.
이해해 줘.

Take care of your health.

mom joshimhae.
mohm joe-shim-hay.
몸 조심해.

Don't cry!

ulji ma!
ooljee mah!
울지 마!

Wipe your tears!

nunmul dakka!
noon-mool dahkk-ah!
눈물 닦아!

Wait for me.

gidaryeo jwo.
geedah-ryuh jwaw.
기다려 줘.

Peace / be happy

haeng-syo
hang-shyo
행쇼

Popularized by Korea's music/fashion/trend icon G-Dragon, this is a shortened way of saying 행복하십시오 [**haeng bok ha sip syo**], meaning peace / be happy.